Barth for Armchair Theologians

Also Available in the Armchair Series

Barth for Armchair Theologians

JOHN R. FRANKE

ILLUSTRATIONS BY RON HILL

Westminster John Knox Press
LOUISVILLE • LONDON

Scripture quotations from the New Revised Standard Version of the Bible are copyright © 1989 by the Division of Christian Education of the National Council of the Churches of Christ in the U.S.A. and are used by permission.

Book design by Sharon Adams
Cover design by Jennifer K. Cox
Cover illustration by Ron Hill

First edition
Published by Westminster John Knox Press
Louisville, Kentucky

This book is printed on acid-free paper that meets the American National Standards Institute Z39.48 standard. ♾

PRINTED IN THE UNITED STATES OF AMERICA

07 08 09 10 11 12 13 14 15—10 9 8 7 6 5 4 3 2

Library of Congress Cataloging-in-Publication Data is on file at the Library of Congress, Washington, D.C.

ISBN-13: 978-0-664-22734-0
ISBN-10: 0-664-22734-1

For J. J.
(because this one has pictures)

Contents

Introduction   ix

1. Embracing Liberal Theology   1

2. Breaking with Liberalism   21

3. A New Theology   39

4. The Impossible Possibility   57

5. Bearing Christian Witness   79

6. *Church Dogmatics*   99

7. Barth's Legacy   149

Notes   167

For Further Reading   173

Index   177

INTRODUCTION

When future historians look back on developments in the discipline of theology over the course of the twentieth century, there is little doubt that Karl Barth will tower above the others as the most prominent and influential theologian of his time. His thought was a decisive influence in changing the direction of theology in Europe and North America and continues to provide a fruitful resource for those seeking alternatives to the standard liberal and conservative approaches to theology that have been so influential and polarizing in the Anglo-American setting. In addition, his theology has found resonance with Christian thinkers around the world and continues to be the focal point of much study and conversation. In the midst of this ongoing engagement with his thought, Barth has come to be considered by many not simply as the outstanding voice of the twentieth century, but also as one of the most significant theologians in the history of the Christian church.

Yet in many ways much of this interest has been focused primarily in the context of the academy rather than in the church. This is perhaps understandable given the sheer size of Barth's magnum opus, the *Church Dogmatics* (nearly eight thousand pages in the English translation), and the complex and often counterintuitive nature of his thought. It would be easy to assume that an advanced degree in theology is necessary in order to even attempt to read Barth, much less to navigate his writings and ideas with any degree of genuine comprehension and benefit. However, this assumption is not in keeping with Barth's intentions. Indeed, although he spent most of his career teaching theology in a university setting, he came to consider the Christian church to be his primary audience and wrote to assist that particular community in its proclamation of the gospel of Jesus Christ. He was always most delighted to hear about the influence of his work in the life and ministry of the church. In other words, Barth was no ivory-tower theologian. Instead he was passionate about the relationship of theology to life, reportedly suggesting that Christian preaching and teaching should be done with the Bible in one hand and today's newspaper in the other.

This little book tells the story of Barth's theological journey from liberalism to a new form of theology. He sought to resist the assumptions and conclusions of liberal theology while at the same time avoiding the temptation to simply return to some supposedly pristine, premodern form of Christian orthodoxy. Instead, Barth took the intellectual traditions of the Enlightenment and Protestant orthodoxy with the utmost seriousness while at the same time subjecting both to critical scrutiny. The result is an approach to theology that is deeply immersed in the Bible and the faith of the church while also being significantly engaged with the questions and challenges of contemporary life and thought. This approach to theology has provided hope and inspiration to many people who have struggled to hold the commitments of their faith together with the realities of the modern world. At the same time, it has also drawn the ire and criticism of others who think that it remains either too conservative, as with many liberals, or too liberal, as with many conservatives. Here readers are invited to enter into this story for themselves and to come to their own conclusions.

John R. Franke
Hatfield, Pennsylvania
Advent 2005

CHAPTER ONE

Embracing Liberal Theology

Karl Barth was born in the Swiss city of Basel on May 10, 1886, to parents who were steeped in the traditions of Christian faith and its theological expression. His mother, Anna, was the daughter of a pastor and the descendant of a family of whom many had been involved in the work of ministry and academics. His father, Fritz, had earned a degree in theology and was a teacher at the College of Preachers in Basel. Three years after Karl's birth, the family moved to Bern when his father accepted an offer to teach at the university. Fritz Barth was an advocate of a moderate form of conservative Protestantism that was known at the time as positive theology. In addition, Fritz had been strongly influenced by Pietism and believed that while doctrine was important, genuine Christian experience was to be more highly valued, to such an extent that he regarded orthodoxy as something of a negative influence on the vibrancy of the Christian life. Hence, the Barth home was filled with conversation concerning the meaning and implications of the Christian faith coupled with an emphasis on piety and Christian experience that was deemed to be an appropriate expression of Christian belief. In this context it is hardly surprising that young Karl developed an interest in theology.

His decision to engage in the formal study of theology occurred in the context of his confirmation classes in 1901–1902, and upon completing his schooling two years later he began his theological studies at the University of Bern. After four semesters at Bern, Karl followed the tradition of many Swiss theological students and continued his studies in Germany, moving on to the University of Berlin and then to Tübingen before finishing up at the University of Marburg. Upon completing his theological examinations back in Switzerland, he returned to Marburg for one more year before entering the pastorate.

In the midst of all this moving about, Karl was engaged in an ongoing debate with his father concerning the direction of his education. After his initial semesters in Bern, Karl wanted to continue his studies at Marburg, a leading center of theological liberalism. His father wanted his son to continue his education in a more conservative setting. The two finally compromised on the University of Berlin. Karl also did another semester at Bern and then, at the insistence of his father, one with the conservative faculty at

Tübingen, which his father hoped would provide Karl with a more conservative theological orientation. In fact, his semester there had the reverse effect, convincing Karl that the conservative approach was not tenable. With one semester of university study remaining, his father finally relented and allowed Karl to attend Marburg.

At Marburg Karl sat under the teaching of Wilhelm Herrmann, one of the leading proponents of progressive Protestant thought in Germany. Barth was already familiar with Herrmann prior to his arrival in Marburg, having encountered his work earlier in his studies with a great deal of admiration. In this setting, as he listened to the teaching

of this esteemed thinker on the subjects of theology and ethics, the young Barth became a firmly convinced disciple of Herrmann and his liberal approach to theology, commenting that he soaked Herrmann in through all of his pores. Among the other professors that Barth encountered was Martin Rade, who was popular with students and known for his friendliness and availability. Barth spent many pleasant hours discussing theology in the context of the open evenings for students that Rade hosted at his home on a regular basis. In addition to being a professor of theology, Rade was also the editor of *Die Christliche Welt*, one of the most influential theological journals in Germany at the time. Apparently he was impressed by Barth and appointed him to serve as the editorial assistant for the journal, providing Barth with the opportunity to spend the 1908–1909 academic year in Marburg immersing himself in the theological discussions of the time and gaining valuable experience before entering the pastorate. In order to understand the subsequent events in Barth's life and thought, it is important to grasp something of the character of the liberal theology that he came to embrace and promote at Marburg. In attempting to understand the concerns of liberal theology, we must look back approximately 250 years prior to the beginning of the twentieth century, to the middle of the seventeenth century and the emergence of one of the most significant and far-reaching periods of Western intellectual and cultural history.

The Enlightenment

The common ways in which men and women in the West thought about God, themselves, and the world in which they lived were forever altered by the Enlightenment, a period of European thought and culture often referred to

as the age of reason. Broadly speaking, the Enlightenment extended from the middle of the seventeenth century through the eighteenth and marked the completion of the transition from the ancient world to the modern that had its beginnings in the Renaissance. One of the most basic shifts in thinking that occurred in the Enlightenment is seen in the elevated status of human beings and their capabilities as compared to the common assumptions of the medieval world, in which God was the central focal point and concern of history. The Enlightenment shifted the focus of history to human beings and their activity, while the significance of the divine was construed in terms of the value of God for the lives of humans.

This elevated status of human beings was coupled with an optimistic outlook concerning their intellectual and moral capabilities that ran contrary to the Christian tradition. Prior to the Enlightenment, divine revelation was considered to be the final arbiter of truth in the knowing process, and the particular focal point of this revelation was the Bible. The role of human reason was simply to seek to comprehend and obey the truth contained in revelation and Scripture. This understanding of knowledge is captured in the medieval assertion that human beings must first believe in order to understand, that true knowledge must begin with faith as the basis for knowing and then seek understanding.

In the Enlightenment, the notion of externally received revelation as the final judge of truth was replaced by internal human reason. In other words, enlightened human beings would no longer be bound by the dictates of any external authority, be it the church or the Bible, that claimed to speak for God. They would follow their own experience and reason wherever it would lead as the means of obtaining knowledge rather than blindly accept what they regarded to be the superstitions proclaimed and taught by traditional Christian faith. Instead of believing in order to understand, the Enlightenment maintained that humans should believe only that which they could understand. Similarly, with respect to morality, it was believed that human reason was able to discover the natural moral law that was internal to all persons and to bring about conformity to this universal natural law for the good of all.

From this perspective, the thinkers of the Enlightenment launched a vigorous and thoroughgoing critique of traditional Christian teachings, such as the deity of Christ, the authenticity of the miracles recorded in the Bible, the idea of divine revelation, the inspiration and authority of Scripture, and the resurrection of Jesus Christ from the dead. In addition, the confidence that abounded in the ability of human reason to provide the practical, moral, and

religious resources necessary for human flourishing apart from the teachings and doctrines of traditional Christian faith, which claimed to be the product of divine revelation, served to marginalize the God of the Bible and the Christian faith in the life and mind of Western culture.

The reliance on human reason instead of divine revelation as the basis for knowledge was seen, from the perspective of the Enlightenment, as the emancipation of human beings from the authority of the church and the Bible that had been characteristic of the medieval world. In this way the Enlightenment was viewed as a crucial stage in the intellectual maturity of human beings in which they learned to think for themselves instead of depending on the Bible and the tradition of the church. Enlightenment thinkers had come to believe that Christianity was largely irrelevant to the issues and concerns of the modern world. As philosopher Immanuel Kant put it, the Enlightenment represents the emergence of human beings from a self-inflicted state of tutelage. Tutelage is the inability to make use of one's understanding without guidance from another. In their emancipation from tutelage, human beings are summoned to demonstrate the courage to make use of their own understanding for the common good. "Dare to know!" This is, according to Kant, the motto of the Enlightenment. On the other hand, others came to view this courage not as the eradication of faith, but instead as the call to another manifestation of faith. As Karl Barth came to characterize the Enlightenment, it was a system of thought founded on the presupposition of faith in the omnipotence of human reason and ability.

In the midst of the unfolding of the Enlightenment, coupled with the response of the church and the proponents of orthodoxy to its critique of traditional Christian beliefs and assumptions, it seemed increasingly clear that thoughtful persons were faced with a fairly unambiguous and stark choice: either cast off Christianity and adopt the outlook of the Enlightenment with its ideals of human autonomy and freedom, or reject this new perspective and continue to be Christian. While one could opt for either Christianity or the Enlightenment, it seemed clear to many that the two perspectives could not be held together in a coherent fashion. However, not everyone accepted that these were the only two possibilities. Among those who objected to the dichotomy between the Enlightenment and Christianity was Friedrich Schleiermacher, the so-called father of modern theology, whose work ushered in a new approach to the Christian faith that seemed to many to breathe new life into the study of theology.

Schleiermacher and the Advent of Liberal Theology

Friedrich Schleiermacher (1768–1834) was the son of an ordained Reformed minister who served as an army chaplain. His parents were devout Christians who had experienced a devotional renewal through contacts with some members of the Moravian Brethren, a prominent group of Pietists that had experienced renewal in the eighteenth century under the leadership of Nikolaus von Zinzendorf. Pietism was a movement that started in Germany in the seventeenth century and sought the revival of personal religion and Christian faith over against the arid and often lifeless doctrinal orthodoxy that had become common among

Protestant churches. Pietist leaders such as Philipp Jacob Spener, August Hermann Francke, and Zinzendorf launched a campaign for renewed urgency and fervor in Bible study, preaching, prayer, and practical ministry that arose from the personal experience of the salvation offered through the gospel and a living and ongoing relationship with Jesus Christ. In addition to this individual experience that characterized Pietism in general, the Moravians were also highly committed to the importance of community and maintained strong communal practices.

The Moravian devotion to the personal and social implications of the gospel led them to become evangelists and missionary pioneers as well as to establish schools, orphanages, and other charitable institutions. While their theology remained traditionally conservative, the Moravian emphasis on personal, inward experience coupled with the communal and social expression of that experience provided a significant alternative to the external formalism of traditional Protestant Christianity as well as to the rationalistic intellectualism of the Enlightenment.

In 1783 Friedrich was sent, along with his brother and sister, to a Moravian boarding school by his parents, who desired that their children should experience and embrace the Christian faith as understood by the Moravians. Friedrich did experience a conversion of sorts among the Moravians. Indeed, the pleasures of rigorous intellectual pursuit in the context of a vital Christian community characterized by warmhearted devotion to Jesus, vibrant worship, and close personal relationships provided the young Schleiermacher with a set of formative religious experiences that influenced him for the rest of his life. Commenting on the significance of these experiences later in his life, he wrote to his sister that he still considered himself a Moravian pietist, only one of a "higher order" due to his willingness to couple religious experience with the intellectual scrutiny and criticism of religious beliefs.

Such scrutiny was important for Schleiermacher because, in spite of the strength of his experience, he continued to struggle with doubts about the veracity of some of the beliefs that he was taught by the Moravians. After he transferred to the Moravian seminary, his letters to his father expressed his growing concerns that his teachers were failing to address the commonly held doubts about traditional Christian teaching that afflicted so many people of his day. He finally confessed that these doubts were his, and that he could not believe that Jesus is the true, eternal God or that his death constituted a substitutionary atonement for human sin. He concluded that the resolution of his doubts could be worked out only in an atmosphere of free critical inquiry and so dropped out of the Moravian seminary and matriculated at the University of Halle, where he immersed himself in the study of theology and contemporary philosophy.

From this background, Schleiermacher went on to forge a new theological paradigm that would come to be called liberalism. In 1799 he published the highly influential work *On Religion: Speeches to its Cultured Despisers*, which maintained that the critics of religion and Christianity had failed to properly grasp the true nature of that which they were rejecting. He argued that Christianity was a religion and, as such, had to be understood on its own terms, beginning with a revised understanding of what constituted a religion. The essence of religion was formed not by outward practices or adherence to particular doctrines, both of which could be assessed externally. Instead, true religion consisted of internal experience and the disposition of piety toward the divine. Hence, religion was to be viewed as distinct from the *knowledge* of the world, the

sphere of science and history, as well as the *activity* in the world, the sphere of morality and ethics. Religion was *feeling*. What makes a person religious was not having thoughts or beliefs about the divine, but experiencing the divine in one's life, having a basic, fundamental awareness of the self in relation to that which is called "God" by some and the "Universe" or the "Sublime" by others.

While Schleiermacher distinguished feeling from knowing and doing, he also asserted that feeling always accompanies knowing and doing. Hence, he argued that it was impossible to be truly scientific and ethical without also being religious. The cultured critics or despisers of religion, in their rejection of it, were therefore depriving themselves of the very resource necessary for the activities of science and morality to which they professed to be committed. This appeal to experience was appropriate for the mood of the time, and intellectuals desired to move beyond the rationalism of the Enlightenment to an engagement with that which was beyond reason. This movement was known as Romanticism, and it entailed both an inward turn to experience as well as an outward turn to the particularities of history, language, and culture. Schleiermacher's conception of religion in the *Speeches on Religion* included both of these concerns through an emphasis on the universal religious impulse of human beings in its various concrete and historical expressions. Christianity represents the expression of this universal religious impulse as it is mediated through the particular language and symbols of the Christian tradition.

The *Speeches on Religion* marked a turning point in the history of Christian theology as the first attempt by a Christian to interpret the faith in relation to the categories and assumptions of modern, post-Enlightenment culture. While Schleiermacher affirmed and embraced many of the common assumptions of the Enlightenment, he also sought to move beyond the limitations of its rationalism by freshly articulating the significance of religion in his day and attempting to rethink the study of Christian theology on the basis of the universal human experience of the divine.

A few years after the publication of the *Speeches on Religion*, Schleiermacher was appointed to a professorship at the University of Halle, where he lectured on philosophy, theology, ethics, and New Testament interpretation. However, after several years he was forced to leave the university and the city when it was occupied by Napoleon's army.

He moved to Berlin, where he accepted the pastorate of Trinity Church in 1809 and helped to establish the new University of Berlin, where he served as professor of theology. In these spheres of activity, Schleiermacher was widely influential as a preacher and a teacher.

The culmination of Schleiermacher's work is *The Christian Faith*, a lengthy and detailed exposition of particularly Christian theology from the perspective of religion first articulated in the *Speeches on Religion*. Published in 1821–22 and again in a revised and final version in 1830, it represents the fruit of years of thoughtful reflection in the context of a life spent in both pastoral and academic

settings. In this work, religious experience or emotion is defined more precisely as "the feeling of absolute dependence" that describes the basic and universal awareness and orientation of individuals toward ultimate reality. From this starting point in religious feeling and experience, the work expounds the distinctively Christian religion that views all things in the light of the experience of redemption found in Christ. While all persons are religious in that all stand in relation to ultimate reality, for Christians this feeling or awareness is made actual and concrete only through a relation to the person of Jesus. Loyalty to Jesus is what defines Christian faith as Christian. Jesus of Nazareth is the one whose consciousness and awareness of God— the feeling of absolute dependence—was unclouded by sin. From this emphasis on Jesus as the focal point of the Christian religious experience, Schleiermacher turns his attention to the whole body of classical Christian teaching and doctrine for the purpose of reinterpreting it in light of the nature of religious feeling and its particular manifestation in Christianity.

The Christian Faith marked a major milestone in the history of theology as well as a significant departure from traditional Christian belief. It created controversy among theologians, some of whom accused Schleiermacher of so altering the Christian faith that he had essentially abandoned it. Others, who believed that the faith had to be revised in the aftermath of the Enlightenment, took up the perspective articulated by Schleiermacher in the *Speeches on Religion* and *The Christian Faith* as well as in his sermons and other works and began to forge a new movement know as liberalism. Schleiermacher's thought provided the touchstone for the development of this liberal school of theology that came to dominate Protestant thought throughout the latter half of the nineteenth century and into the twentieth. Hence, he is known as the father of modern, or liberal, theology.

The Development of Liberal Theology

If the thought of Schleiermacher is the fountainhead of theological liberalism, it was left to others to develop and extend the tradition over the course of the nineteenth century and into the twentieth. One of the most prominent names in this process is that of Albrecht Ritschl (1822–89). Ritschl was the most influential theologian in late-nineteenth-century Ger-

man Protestant thought. He held one of the most distinguished teaching positions in theology at the time and by
the end of his career was acknowledged as the head of a
distinct and diverse school of theological thought known as
"Ritschlianism." For Ritschl, the historical content and
central convictions of Christianity are to be found in the
proclamation of Jesus concerning the kingdom of God.
Jesus is viewed as the bearer of new religious teaching and
as the focal point of the kingdom of God, the concept that
Ritschl used to speak of the new life of the community
which Jesus founded. This community is characterized by
a strongly ethical dimension, which is the chief aspect of
the Christian faith, as opposed to doctrinal or metaphysical
beliefs and concerns. To be Christian is to follow the ethical and moral teaching of Jesus.

While Jesus is at the center of Christianity for Ritschl, he
is not to be viewed as the eternal Son of God incarnate in
human form, as in classical Christian thought. Instead, he
was a human preacher and teacher who could be known
through the study of history apart from the assumptions of
traditional Christian dogma. Ritschl believed that through
the historical investigation of the founding and development of Christianity, our understanding of the human values and ideals that it embodied could be deepened and
extended. Theology involves the historical investigation of
the religious and ethical concerns of the Christian church,
a community that collectively makes the value judgment
that the highest good of humanity is to be found in the
kingdom of God revealed by Jesus Christ. The truth of this
assertion is supported by historical investigation into the
life and teachings of Jesus, who represents the highest
ideals of humanity. In Ritschl's thought, the study of theology seeks to determine the true and enduring essence of
Christianity as something distinct from its outward forms

and expressions that must be discovered through critical historical inquiry.

Ritschl's emphasis on the historical, the communal, and the ethical left no place in his understanding of theology for the individual experience of faith, and he was highly critical of Schleiermacher's experiential theory of religion. The primary concern of religion is not in the realm of feeling and experience, but has to do instead with the will and the determination to live a moral and ethical life. The Christian religion is understood not as a form of experiential or theoretical knowledge, but rather as practical ethical and moral activity. For Ritschl this means that the biblical notion of the kingdom of God is to be interpreted in moral terms such that Christian religion and ethics are viewed as being inextricably bound, with the consequence that Christian faith can be affirmed and verified only in the context of ethics.

One of Ritschl's students was Wilhelm Herrmann (1846–1922). While Herrmann shared Ritschl's disdain for all forms of metaphysics in theology and his emphasis on ethics, he also believed that Ritschl had overstated the ways in which faith was dependent on historical knowledge. Herrmann maintained that religion was distinct from all other realms of human activity and inquiry, including science, history, and ethics. Thus, while he was concerned with each of these areas of thought, he also maintained that none of them were able to demonstrate or verify the truth of religious faith. He believed that religious faith was categorically different from all other forms of knowing, meaning that there was no way to move, for instance, from the world of science to the world of faith. Likewise, since historical research was restricted to the natural world, it could not reveal anything of true religion.

The categorical difference between religious faith and all other forms of knowledge means that for Herrmann, only religious faith could provide certainty and confidence in the centrality of Jesus Christ for Christianity. While science was directed toward that which was provable and demonstrable, religion was directly experienced by the individual. This religious experience was self-authenticating for Herrmann in that it was impossible to provide an answer concerning its reality other than to say that it is known through religion. Confidence in the truth of Christianity comes not through the Bible, the church, or human reason but solely from a direct experience of Christ. Thus, religion can only be truly believed and lived from within; it cannot be justified from the perspective of an external observer. In this way, Herrmann believed that he was able to affirm the basic insights of Ritschl concerning the importance of history and ethics while at the same time returning to the central concerns of Schleiermacher in the *Speeches on Religion*, which he regarded as the most important work since the New Testament.

The perspective of Herrmann triggered significant discussion and criticism among other Ritschlians who believed that his sharp distinction between faith and other forms of knowledge essentially restricted religion to its own privatized context and cut it off from any public discourse and engagement. It was this version of faith-based liberal theology that Karl Barth embraced at Marburg and carried with him into the challenges of pastoral ministry back home in Switzerland. His eventual response to it would decisively alter the theological history of the twentieth century.

CHAPTER TWO

Breaking with Liberalism

Karl Barth began his career by serving as an assistant pastor to the German-speaking Reformed congregation in Geneva from 1909 to 1911. He was installed on September 26 and gave his first sermon. Barth reports that five minutes before he went up into the pulpit to begin his ministry, he received in the mail a copy of the new edition of Herrmann's work on ethics, sent to him by his former teacher. At the time he believed that this coincidence indicated the future direction of his work.

During the following two years Barth's time was taken up almost entirely with his pastoral duties. He devoted particular attention to his sermons, which were usually sixteen pages in length and written out word for word. They were very academic and also quite liberal, in keeping with his outlook on theology and the ministerial vocation. For instance, these early sermons contained remarks such as the following: "the greatest thing is what takes place in our hearts"; "Calvin's view of the authority of the Bible would be quite wrong for us"; "Sometimes they [the Ten Commandments] contain too much for our needs and sometimes too little." In one sermon he maintained that "James wrote the section we are looking at now in a weak moment"; he also dismissed the orthodox understanding of Christ articulated in the Chalcedonian Definition, commenting that "if Jesus were like this I would not be interested in him."[1]

In Geneva, Barth's sermons were frequently delivered in the auditorium and from the pulpit where the Protestant reformer John Calvin had lectured and preached. Barth later remarked that Calvin would hardly have been pleased at the sermons he preached from his pulpit. At the time, however, Barth was fully confident concerning his teaching, describing himself as a completely convinced liberal who "knew everything, and knew it better than anyone else," who taught and preached with "unshakeable confidence."[2] After two years as an assistant pastor, Barth moved to the small Swiss village of Safenwil in the summer of 1911, where he spent the next ten years of his life as pastor of the local parish church.

The "Red" Pastor of Safenwil

The years in Safenwil were among the most formative of Barth's life. His thinking was shaped and transformed in the context of his pastoral work, eventually leading to a change of mind and heart with respect to the proper direction for theology. Several factors precipitated Barth's famous

"break with liberalism." The most important of these is clearly the outbreak of World War I in August 1914. However, even before this calamitous event, Barth was feeling increasingly estranged from the worldview assumptions that fueled his liberal professors and their students. During his early years in Safenwil, Barth was exposed to the Swiss social democratic movement, which was then at its height, and over the years he grew increasingly concerned with the plight of the working class. His extensive engagement with local social and political questions and his reading of leading Christian social thinkers led to his longing for a new world, a new social order that would put a stop to the oppression of the poor and disenfranchised and challenge the well-to-do to take seriously the social responsibilities of their privileged position.

In the later half of the nineteenth century, socialism spread and gained increasing acceptance throughout Europe. From the very beginning of the movement, there were Christians who believed that the practice of socialism constituted the outworking of Christian theory. Hence, while socialism has often been associated with the communism and official atheism of Soviet Russia, there were from the beginning Christians who were committed to socialism in the context of the Christian faith. Barth found some forms of Christian socialism problematic because of their thinly veiled or explicit nationalism. However, other forms were more interesting to the new pastor, such as those that were related to the vision of Johann and Christoph Blumhardt. The Blumhardts were pietists who were dissatisfied with the focus on the salvation of individuals for a heavenly future that had been characteristic of the tradition. They maintained that the message of the gospel and the early Christians was not the promise of salvation in some other world, but rather the coming of God's new creation to the present world. This led to a deep conviction concerning the necessity of the social embodiment of the gospel. The Christian message did not simply promise a future life in another world, but made a profound difference in present circumstances through its announcement of the coming of the kingdom of God to the earth. The focal point of this movement was hope in the possibility of a visible and tangible appearance of the kingdom of God and the lordship of Jesus Christ in the world. Christoph Blumhardt became active in social democratic politics and was elected to the regional parliament while continuing to exercise powerful influence on the church, leading to the growth of a religious socialism in Switzerland that remained distinctively Christian.

While the Blumhardts had a significant influence on the development of religious socialism in Switzerland, the two leading figures of the movement were Herrmann Kutter and Leonhard Ragaz. Kutter, a pastor in Zurich, had provided the impetus for religious socialism through his preaching and writing, which were deeply influenced by the work of Marx and contemporary Marxists. He viewed the emergence of socialism as a secular version of a new world that pointed to the kingdom of God proclaimed by Jesus. He believed that in spite of the fact that socialists were often atheists, they were nevertheless powerfully

engaged in the struggle to oppose the existing powers of the world that caused the oppression, misery, and suffering of so many of its inhabitants. On the other hand, the church, by virtue of the easy and comfortable relationship it maintained with the existing order, suggested that the God of whom the church spoke was an impotent God who either accepted the current situation or was powerless to change it. Over against the charge that the socialists were materialists, Kutter maintained that while often this was true, it also produced the conviction that existing conditions could be changed to reflect a more just and equitable society. In suggesting that existing material conditions could not be changed, the church demonstrated the degree to which it supported and was in fact itself dependent on the very conditions that produced such miserable and hopeless oppression in the lives of so many.

This outlook inclined Kutter to let socialism take its course without interference and opposition from the church. He believed that secular Marxism might even be an instrument of God in helping to call the church from its slumber and bring about a new world. At the same time, he was not interested in politics and believed that while the church should repent of its complacency and reform its ways, it should not join with atheistic socialists in the pursuit of a common social agenda. Ragaz, a pastor in Basel and the other leading figure in the movement, took a different view. He was by nature an activist and believed that secular social democracy was the precursor to the kingdom of God. Therefore, he maintained that the church should be actively involved in the promotion of religious socialism as well as seek an alliance with the secular socialists in the relentless pursuit of an alternative society. This difference in perspective created tensions in the movement. Kutter believed that it was useless to attempt to "baptize" social democracy, since only Christians could truly understand the message and implications of the gospel. Therefore he opposed the idea of working with the socialists to see how they might contribute to the work of the church and believed that Ragaz was advocating entering into alliances that would dilute the distinctive message of the Christian gospel. Ragaz, on the other hand, found Kutter's reluctance to work with the socialists to be misguided and shortsighted. While he also was critical of aspects of Marxism, he believed that direct involvement with the socialists was the most effective way to bring about true societal change and to correct the problems of Marxism. This tension eventually led to a split in the movement, triggered by the outbreak of war.

Barth's engagement with the struggles and challenges of his parishioners led him to read and study the literature of religious socialism with profound effect. He noted that the class conflict which he saw before him in his congregation forced him to confront, for the first time, the real problems of life. Hence, for a period of time, his theological work included serious study and engagement with factory acts, safety laws, and trade unionism as his attention was claimed by the local struggles of the working class. During this time Barth not only became a convinced socialist but he also came to see an intimate connection between the ideas of religious socialism and the gospel itself, asserting that the social movement of the nineteenth and twentieth centuries was both the "greatest and most urgent word of God" in the present time as well as a "direct continuation of the spiritual power" which entered into the history and life of the world through the person and message of Jesus. Barth gave numerous addresses and lectures on socialism and conducted evening classes for workers to help them understand their situation and to provide practical assistance. In addition to earning him the epithet the "red" pastor of Safenwil, Barth's socialist commitments coupled with his immersion in the struggles of his working-class parishioners also had the effect of eroding his confidence in the bourgeois religious ethos and assumptions of liberalism and alienating him from the intellectual context and mindset that shaped his teachers. While this did not lead Barth to abandon liberal theology, it did unsettle him and lead to some modifications in his thinking as well as providing the fertile soil in which a full-scale departure from his earlier ideas became possible if not inevitable.

The Great War and the End of Liberal Theology

Everything changed for Barth with the dramatic and tragic events of August 1914 and the beginning of the Great War. Coming to terms with the outbreak of war was difficult enough, but Barth was shocked to discover that his former teachers had signed a declaration of support for the kaiser and the war. He concluded that their submission to the ideology of war left them and the theology that they espoused "hopelessly compromised." Years later Barth recalled his extreme dismay at this turn of events and the collapse of his intellectual world:

> One day in early August 1914 stands out in my personal memory as a black day. Ninety-three German intellectuals impressed public opinion by their proclamation in support of the war policy of Wilhelm II and his counselors. Among these intellectuals I discovered to my horror almost all of my theological teachers whom I had greatly venerated. In despair over what this indicated about the signs of the time I suddenly realized that I could not any longer follow either their ethics and dogmatics or their understand-

ing of the Bible and of history. For me at least, 19th-century theology no longer held any future.[3]

Barth considered this support of the war to be nothing less than a betrayal of the Christian faith made possible by liberal theology. In a letter to his former mentor Martin Rade, the editor of *Die Christliche Welt,* which came out in support of the war, he wrote that the saddest development of the religious justification of the war that appeared in the pages of the journal was the way in which the love of the Fatherland, the assumption of the legitimacy of war, and the Christian faith were brought together in "hopeless confusion" across Germany. Since the journal appeared to Barth to promote this situation, he concluded that it had ceased to be Christian at the precise hour in which German history and culture was most in need of Christian witness and had instead aligned itself with the concerns and aspirations of the world. In retrospect, Barth commented that for him this represented the end of liberal theology: "An entire world of theological exegesis, ethics, dogmatics, and preaching, which up to that point I had accepted as basically credible, was thereby shaken to the foundations, and with it everything which flowed at that time from the pens of the German theologians."[4]

For Barth, the fatal flaw in the liberal approach to theology was its limited ability to speak about God in ways that challenged the assumptions and presuppositions of a particular culture. While liberals could speak with conviction concerning matters such as religion, history, culture, and ethics, their approach to theology did not provide them with the necessary resources to speak about God in ways that called into question and challenged the status

quo. Hence, the God of liberal theology appeared to Barth to function as one who simply sanctioned the values and norms that society had established and certified them with a divine seal of approval. Such a view also assumes that God and human beings exist in an essentially common context with a fairly stable relationship. It was difficult to see how, given liberal assumptions, one could conclude that God opposed the values, ideals, and aspirations of a particular cultural setting. Hence, the residents of the competing nations of "Christian" Europe simply assumed that God was on their side and that God sanctioned their nationalistic concerns for "Christian civilization," even to the point of affirming the legitimacy of war to attain their goals.

Barth concluded that such ideas were blasphemous and simply amounted to equating talk about humanity and human culture with talk about God. Put another way, liberal talk about God was merely talk about humanity with a louder voice. Alternatively, Barth increasingly believed that to speak of God was to speak of something different, strange, and startling. God does not come to us in ways that simply affirm what we already believe and practice as a matter of course, but God comes to us and speaks to us on God's own terms, invading and disrupting what we have known and take for granted by calling into being a new reality that we could not have foreseen or imagined. This outlook had a profound effect on Barth's conception of preaching. How was he supposed to fulfill his pastoral duty and obligation to preach the word of God when all he had to offer were human words? He had once been utterly confident in his preaching, but the idea started to fill him with distress at his inadequacy. What did he really have to say to his congregation? Later in life, Barth often made reference to his increasing terror at the prospect of preaching as a significant factor in his break with liberalism.

In addition to the capitulation of his liberal teachers to the ideology of war, Barth was also disheartened to find that the religious socialist movement in which he had seen such promise had also largely followed this path. In addition, he had questions about the options available in religious socialism. He appreciated aspects of the positions of both Kutter and Ragaz. He affirmed Kutter's assertion that the church should be cautious about aligning with any political ideology or program, since these should never be confused with the kingdom of God. However, in spite of the potential dangers, concrete action was required, and Kutter's constant critique of all the options and possibilities meant that he never seemed to propose a plan of action. On the other hand, he appreciated the challenge of Ragaz to put principles into action in spite of the risks. But he also believed that Ragaz had not been alert to the attendant dangers in aligning Christianity with socialism. Barth himself had become more cautious about identifying socialism with the kingdom, and concluded that continuing to pursue the agenda of religious socialism was no longer an option, particularly in light of its failure to resist supporting the war.

This disappointment, coupled with the loss of the liberal theology that had shaped and formed him along with the approach to pastoral ministry that it entailed, triggered in Barth an intense period of intellectual reflection on his life and commitments. What was the way forward? Was any hope to be found in the Christian faith? He spent much of this period in conversation and dialogue with his close friend Eduard Thurneysen, who was also a pastor in a nearby village. Together they debated theology and politics in the confines of neutral Switzerland while the war raged all around them. They concluded that what was needed could not be construed from the options that they perceived to be currently available, such as theological liberalism or religious socialism, but rather something "totally different" or "totally other" was necessary that could serve as the basis for a new world. With that thought in mind, they committed themselves to a renewed engagement with the Bible.

The Strange New World of the Bible

In their search for a new world, Barth and Thurneysen turned to the Bible in the hope of finding some wisdom that they had previously overlooked. "More reflectively than ever before we began reading and expounding the writings of the Old and New Testaments. And behold, they began to speak to us—very differently than we had supposed we were obliged to hear them speak in the school of

what was then called 'modern' [liberal] theology."[5] As this suggests, this intensive reading and study of Scripture led Barth to rethink the nature of the Bible. Liberal thinkers believed that common human religious experience could enable them to determine what in the Bible is simply cultural custom or bias and what constitutes abiding, universal truth. This placed the focus on the human authorship of Scripture, in which the Bible was seen as the product of fallible humans who were conditioned and limited by their times, while still rising to great heights of expression under the illumination of the presence of God.

Because the Bible was not viewed as the word of God in the strict sense, liberals suggested that readers of Scripture must discriminate between the word of God and the words of human beings. This did not mean that the Bible was unimportant for liberal theologians. While the Bible remained extremely important, more attention was given to its contents as a collection of symbolic documents rather than historical ones. The liberal turn to religious experience led to an innovative proposal as to the nature and function of Scripture. While the Bible was viewed as a human book, it nevertheless remained unique in its witness to the encounter with God in the early faith community. Although these experiences were written long ago in the thought forms and categories of ancient cultures, they were still able to speak to diverse and contemporary societies due to their connection to common and universal human experiences that remain the same throughout human existence in every time, place, and culture. Therefore, the task of the contemporary biblical interpreter involved seeking the common human experiences that shape the biblical writings and then reframing and reformulating their meaning in ways that are intelligible to modern persons.

Barth came to believe that this approach inevitably led not only to the domestication of the Bible and its message, but also to the domestication of the God to whom the Scriptures bear witness. Increasingly, he came to believe that the Bible pointed to a world beyond that envisioned by theological liberalism or religious socialism. Consequently, he

became more and more intent on pursuing this "strange new world" that he viewed as the only hope for delivering the church and society from the chaos arising from the failure of conservative and progressive or revolutionary proposals and counterproposals. While this "strange new world" is rooted in the context of contemporary and material realities and concerns, and hence does not constitute a denial or repudiation of the concerns of religious socialism, it is also characterized by a fervent future hope that looks forward with eager anticipation to the new creation promised in the Bible, the world called into being by God. It called for a way of reading the Bible that was more focused on God than that suggested in liberalism with its starting point in human experience.

The Bible is not primarily about history, religion, morality, and the like, but rather God. God is the content of the Bible. It is not right human thoughts about God that make up the content of the Bible, but rather right divine thoughts about human beings. To be led by the Bible into this new world means turning to God anew and learning to follow God's will in the realization that God's will is not merely an improved continuation of ours that can be easily ascertained from our situation. Rather, it stands over against our knowledge and will as something Wholly Other. For Barth, the new world of the Bible "projects itself into our ordinary world. We may say, It is nothing; this is imagination, madness, this 'God.' But we may not deny nor prevent our being led by Bible 'history' far out beyond what is elsewhere called 'history'—into a new world, the world of God."[6]

These convictions about the Bible decisively influenced Barth's thinking in a clear direction. "Over and above the problems associated with liberal theology and Religious Socialism, I began to be increasingly preoccupied with the idea of the kingdom of God in the biblical, real, this-worldly sense of the term. This raised more and more problems over the way in which I should use the Bible in my sermons, which for all too long I had taken for granted."[7]

Hence, in the summer of 1916, Barth turned his attention to an intensive study of the Epistle to the Romans, resulting in a commentary that would not only signal his break with liberalism but also usher in a new conception of theology.

CHAPTER THREE

A New Theology

Barth's break with liberalism and his discovery of the strange new world in the Bible led him on a passionate quest to rethink and reconstruct his understanding of Christian theology, to envision something that could bring about the new world he so fervently sought over the course of his years in the pastorate at Safenwil. He focused his attention on the Epistle to the Romans, and, in the midst of his ongoing pastoral work, he read and read and wrote and wrote. The result of this labor was a large collection of notes on the epistle that were written with what Barth himself called "a joyful sense of discovery."[1] He transformed his notes into the first edition of a commentary on Romans, completed in 1918 and published in 1919. In this work we see the fruit of Barth's theological restlessness in the aftermath of liberalism as well as the constructive insights of his theological imagination worked out in detail for the first time. He continued his work on Romans and completed a second edition of the commentary in 1921. Barth's work on Romans rocked the theological world by challenging many of its core assumptions and calling into question the entire enterprise as it had come to be conceived, particularly in liberal theology. In its aftermath, things would never look quite the same. Barth had done nothing less than written a new theology in the form of a biblical commentary.

Commentary on Romans

Reading Barth's commentary on Romans can be a bit of a shock for contemporary readers who are accustomed to thinking of the commentary genre as a fairly detached and neutral academic exercise. As is generally the case in this approach, commentators subject the text under consideration to critical and historical scrutiny in an attempt to ascertain its precise meaning and its potential significance for an audience well removed from the original time of composition. Barth turns this procedure—in which readers ask questions of the text—on its head, and instead seeks to allow the epistle, as a witness to the gospel of God, to question and judge its readers, calling them, and all of us, into question before the living God. We do not question and judge God, but rather God questions and judges us. Throughout the work Barth presses these issues again and again, stressing the distinction between God, the Lord and Creator, and human beings, who are the creatures of God.

While Barth acknowledges the usefulness of modern methods of biblical interpretation and the value of biblical scholarship, he also makes clear that these are not of primary significance in the task of reading and listening to God speak through the Bible. In the preface to the first edition, Barth remarks that the historical-critical method of biblical investigation has its rightful place in the study of the Bible, since it is concerned with "the preparation of intelligence—and this can never be superfluous." However, in spite of its important role in reading the Bible, it is clearly of secondary significance. Barth writes: "But, were I driven to choose between it and the venerable doctrine of Inspiration, I should without hesitation adopt the latter, which has a broader, deeper, more important justification. The doctrine of Inspiration is concerned with the labour of apprehending, without which no technical equipment, however complete, is of any use whatever." What is most important is not simply a proper knowledge of the historical and cultural details that led to the composition of the

biblical writings, or the critical issues that surround the reception of the text, or even a precise comprehension of its grammatical and syntactical features. What is of supreme significance in the reading of Scripture is apprehending the voice and will of God. Scholarship is useful to this end, but cannot in any way be seen as replacing or eclipsing the inspiration of the Bible. "Fortunately, I am not compelled to choose between the two. Nevertheless, my whole energy of interpretation has been expended in an endeavor to see through and beyond history into the Spirit of the Bible, which is the Eternal Spirit."[2]

This attempt "to see through and beyond history into the spirit of the Bible" gave the work a very different feel than more traditional commentaries, leading some critics to charge that it was little more than an attempt at freestyle theology, an effort to read into the text what he wanted to say and then to try and tie it back to the Bible. Barth addresses this concern in the preface to the second edition, explaining his approach: "I know that I have laid myself open to the charge of imposing a meaning upon the text rather than extracting its meaning from it, and that my method implies this." However, he replies that to the extent that he has a system of interpretation to guide his work, it is limited to the recognition of what the Danish philosopher Søren Kierkegaard referred to as the "infinite qualitative distinction" between time and eternity, between God and human beings. This distinction has both negative and positive significance for the tasks of theology and interpretation and may be succinctly summarized: "God is in heaven, humans are on the earth" and "world remains world but God is God." For Barth, the relationship between the infinite God and created, finite human beings is "the theme of the Bible and the essence of philosophy."[3] Hence, one of the chief concerns of the Romans commentary, and of Barth's theology, is to demonstrate how these truths about God and human beings could be brought into an appropriate relationship with each other while at the same time properly maintaining and ensuring the absolute and fundamental difference that exists between them. God is in heaven, we are on the earth.

It is important to observe that Barth speaks of a relationship between God and humanity as well as a difference. While he clearly and forcefully asserts the crucial nature of the difference between God and humanity, of which we

must be ever mindful in our talk about God, it is also true that Barth had little interest in abstract talk about God that was not related to human beings. The Bible depicts a dramatic engagement between God and human beings which is initiated by God, but which also involves genuine human response and action. This interaction is part and parcel of the covenantal relationship God initiates and establishes with human creatures. Barth depicts the challenge of theology as that of speaking in ways that are an appropriate and necessary part of this covenantal relationship without blurring the distinction that must be kept in place if we are to be faithful participants in this relationship. We must speak about and serve God in ways that are proper to both our status as finite creatures and God's status as infinite Creator. God is in heaven, we are on the earth.

Where the human engagement in this covenantal relationship fails to maintain the necessary difference between God and human beings, and thus confuses the Creator-creature distinction, the result is ungodliness and idolatry that brings forth the judgment of the living God. These themes occupy a significant place in the commentary because they are important in the first three chapters of the epistle. Indeed, Barth titles his treatment of Rom. 1:18–32 "The Night" to underscore the picture of human beings under the judgment of God. One of Barth's points is to remind his readers that God is not bound to the world. God can judge the world. God can withdraw divine favor and presence from the world and its inhabitants. God is free and therefore not a natural part of the created order that is available at the beck and call of humanity. Human beings have no inherent right or claim on God, and they are in no position to manipulate God to serve their own ends. This was Barth's major criticism of those who endorsed the outbreak of war in the name of God: the all-too-ready assumption that God could easily be annexed to the desires, goals, and aspirations of human interest. This assumption cut against one of the central themes of the Bible, the freedom of God, and is tied to the rise of conceptual forms of idolatry. In several respects Barth's commentary on Romans can be understood as an extended reflection on the meaning and implications of the first of the Ten Commandments, "You will have no other gods before me."

One of the chief places where Barth identified contemporary idolatry was in the practice of "religion." It is particularly in religion that we see most pointedly the tendency to confuse the distinction between God and human beings. Human beings desire power and security along with an assurance that their activities and pursuits are

right and above reproach. In order to secure a sense of divine blessing, human beings create gods in their own image from the resources of their own imaginations and create religion to serve the gods they have made. Religion is then pressed into the service of its creators in order to provide justification, sanction, and self-legitimation for their decisions and actions. Even a cursory reading of human religious history, Christian and otherwise, provides numerous examples of such attempts at justification and self-legitimation along with the establishment of power and oppression that often attends to it. When human beings talk about God in such a way as to make their beliefs and aspirations the locus of ultimate truth or to claim divine sanction for institutions that are all too human and flawed, they become guilty of idolatry and ungodliness.

Barth maintained that the Bible legitimatizes only one truth, one story, and one kingdom, the kingdom of God. In the process it delegitimizes every human institution, including the Christian church, precisely because they are not, at the end of the day, the embodiment of the kingdom of God. In his critique of religion, Barth describes it as a disease and sickness that draws human attention and contemplation away from the living God to a divine substitute that is false and tyrannical, promising peace, hope, and prosperity but leading instead to the deformation of humanity and ultimately to the judgment of God. In light of the positive assessment and centrality of religion in the development and shape of liberal theology, Barth's diatribe against it can fairly be described as explosive.

While he was scathing in his view of religion, Barth could also acknowledge that the apparent universality of the human religious impulse demonstrated the inability of human beings to dispense with their Creator. While religion, as a human construction, is utterly unable to provide true knowledge of God, it does serve as a reminder that human beings are designed for a covenantal relationship with God. Hence, while the practice of religion is a destructive mistake, its presence in the world bears witness, of a negative sort, that human beings were made for God and are compelled, in spite of their inadequacy, to bear witness and give glory to God.

The question to be explored was *how* to bear witness and give glory to God without blurring the Creator-creature distinction and lapsing into religion. In order to pursue this task, Barth develops a dialectical approach to human language and speech about God. He speaks of the revelation of God in Jesus Christ as the center of human knowledge of God and yet also asserts that human beings do not have the ability to understand what has been revealed. Hence, Barth can speak of the revelation of God that occurred in Jesus Christ as being like the aftermath of an explosion of an artillery shell. We discern from the large crater that is left behind that something significant has happened, but we are unable to make sense of it within the framework of

the knowledge and experience available to us. The way of life that is ours through the cross of Christ leading to our adoption as God's children comes only through the death of the present world, including us. Further, our adoption as God's children is something that can be grasped only as a promise and not as a possession that can be asserted and assured. For Barth, as soon as we begin to take the promises of God as possessions that have been given to us, we return, however well intended, to the dangers and perils of religion.

Barth's dialectical approach to speaking about God meant that standard assumptions concerning theology, in both liberal and conservative traditions, had to be rethought and reconstructed. Hence, Barth tended to be wary of straightforward propositional statements about God, revelation, and truth which would suggest that we as human creatures are in a position to speak knowingly about things that are of necessity, because of the Creator-creature distinction, known only to God in spite of revelation. Propositions are too static for speech about God. Yet he also wanted to affirm, indeed felt compelled to affirm, that God had indeed been revealed and made known in Jesus Christ. Hence it was necessary to do two things: first, to recognize and acknowledge the inadequacy of human language with respect to God; and second, given the necessity and responsibility of human beings to bear witness to their Creator, to rethink and redeploy patterns of theological speech that were dynamic and more reflective of a God who cannot be pinned down, contained, or put in a box.

Barth's commentary on Romans made a powerful impact on the theological world, perhaps similar to his crater analogy concerning revelation. Those who read the work knew that it represented something new, different, and significant, but many were not yet sure what to make

of it. Indeed, it was subsequently described as landing like a bomb on the playground of theologians. The work clearly called for a new conception of theology and set forth, at least implicitly, an agenda for further study and reflection. However, it also left many questions that needed to be answered and contained a number of issues that Barth would feel the need to refine over the years through further revision of the commentary as well as in a volumi-nous set of writings, including books, articles, and addresses. What did not change was Barth's commitment to the sort

49

of dialectical theology he envisioned in the commentary. He clearly affirmed that the immediate presence and blessing of God is never the secure possession of human beings. As creatures we cannot presume upon God, we cannot "have" God. Instead, we are always in a place of need and dependence on God for our knowledge of God, our speech about God, and our relationship with God. Dialectical theology as Barth envisioned it acknowledges the inadequacy of human language with respect to God, but also the necessity of bearing witness. He succinctly and memorably described the situation as follows: "As ministers we ought to speak of God. We are human, however, and so cannot speak of God. We ought therefore to recognize both *our obligation and our inability* and by that very recognition give God the glory."[4] In order to articulate this insight more fully, Barth would soon turn his attention to teaching and the theological discipline known as dogmatics.

The Tambach Lecture

In the aftermath of the First World War, the political and economic situation in Germany was highly unstable, leading a significant number of German pastors and theologians to begin to search for new directions for the church and theology that were able to address the bewildering concerns facing the German people. A group of German religious socialists formed to respond to the circumstances of postwar Germany, and at their first meeting they determined to hold a conference in Tambach, a small village in Thuringia, in which they would bring together a number of speakers to address the situation. The views of this group were fairly diverse, but they found common ground in their interest in religious socialism, which was more devel-

oped and established in Switzerland than in Germany. This being the case, the organizers of the conference naturally turned to the Swiss for speakers. At the time Karl Barth was not widely known in Germany; his Romans commentary had just been published and had as yet received little notice in Germany. Among those who did know of him, he was thought to be a follower of Ragaz, who had been invited to be one of the major speakers. Barth's perceived connection to Ragaz did elicit an invitation to speak at the conference, which he turned down. However, shortly before the conference, Ragaz decided to remain in Switzerland to attend to developments at home, and Barth was asked to take his place.

Of course, Barth had long since departed from the views

of religious socialism. His address, titled "The Christian in Society," as assigned by the conference planners, turned out to be a sustained critique of the basic principles and assumptions of religious socialism instead of a sympathetic explanation of them. He remarks at the outset of the lecture that the "thought of the Christian's place in society fills one with a curious blend of hope and questioning."[5] The hope relates to the identification of the Christian in society as Christ and not as us. "*The Christian*: we must be agreed that we do *not* mean *the Christians*, not the multitude of the baptized, nor the chosen few who are concerned with Religion and Social Relations, nor even the cream of the noblest and most devoted Christians we might think of: the Christian is *the Christ*."[6] The questioning relates to the current situation of society and the concern: is Christ in us and in today's society? Barth says that we hesitate to answer this question because we know all too well the ways in which Christ and society appear to stand in total antithesis to each other.

The reason for this antithesis concerns the nature of both God and society in turn. God because, as we have seen from the Romans commentary, God is living and distinct from the world and cannot be controlled or reduced to a set of propositions or principles for the good of society. "The Divine is something whole, complete in itself, a kind of new and different something in contrast to the world. It does not permit of being applied, stuck on, and fitted in. It does not permit of being divided and distributed, for the very reason that it is more than religion." The nature of the living God does not allow for "usage" of human beings for their own ends. "Where then has the world of God any available connection with our social life?" Hence, all attempts at something like Christian socialism or religious socialism amount to an attempt to secularize God and Christ,

to take into human hands that which is so distinctly other. Barth says that we must resist this temptation, for "we do not wish to betray him another time."[7]

"And on the other hand we have *society*, also a whole in itself, broken within, perhaps, but outwardly solid—without connections with the kingdom of heaven."[8] Society moves forward according to its own political and economic rules and regulations. And these rules govern society quite apart from the concerns of the kingdom of God. In other words, attempting to open up society and bring it to Christ is not humanly possible. Human beings would have no more success in bringing society to Christ than they would at bringing Christ to society. In light of this state of affairs, the only possible answer is to let God be God. It is God's help that we need, and we will "deceive" society about this reality "if we set to work building churches and chapels and do not learn to wait upon God in a wholly new way." We must learn to wait because "God alone can save the world."[9]

Hence, concerning the theme of the Christian in society, Barth finds a "great promise, a light from above which is shed upon our situation" and also "an unhappy separation, a thoroughgoing opposition between two dissimilar magnitudes."

Both must be kept clearly in sight, for they constitute our hope and our need. Concerning a solution to this antithesis, Barth exclaimed that neither he nor anyone else could provide a solution, for the only possible solution is God alone.[10] God has addressed this intractable situation, which could not be addressed from the human side, in the resurrection of Jesus from the dead, through which the wholly other, eternal life of God has been revealed. In light of the resurrection, human beings can no longer live under the

A New Theology

illusion that we can change the world for God or on behalf of God, but we can live in the assurance that God can and will overcome and transform the world and bring about the kingdom of God. This is our hope.

Therefore, what the Christian can do in society is nothing other than to follow attentively the movement of God. In this following, through word and deed, it is important to remember that the action is God's and not ours, and that our "position" in this following of the movement of God is always "an instant in a *movement*, and any view of it is comparable to the momentary view of a bird in flight. Aside from the movement it is absolutely meaningless, incomprehensible, and impossible." Therefore this "movement" is not of human origin, and cannot be reduced to human comprehension; it is rather "a movement from above, a movement from a third dimension," by which Barth means "the movement of God in history or, otherwise expressed, the movement of God in consciousness, the movement whose power and import are revealed in the resurrection of Jesus Christ from the dead. This must be the gist of all our thinking about the Christian's place in society, whether that thinking arises from hope, from need, or from both alike."[11] Further, and of particular importance, this movement of God must never be identified with the human phenomenon known as religion. "Our concern is *God*, the movement originating in *God*, the motion which *he* leads us—and it is not religion. Hallowed be *thy* name. *Thy* kingdom come. *Thy* will be done. The so-called 'religious experience' is a wholly derived, secondary, fragmentary form of the divine."[12] Hence, while Christians are called to bear witness to God by trying to describe the movement of God, they must also take pains to remind those who listen that what they describe is not the same as its reality.

The Tambach lecture, delivered in September 1919, had a powerful effect on those who heard it, and everyone was aroused by it in one way or another, some in support and others in opposition. In either case, Barth's address had captivated the audience. As one observer remarked, "In comparision with him, all other remarks and discussions faded into insignificance."[13] The lecture made Barth famous overnight and opened doors into Germany for him that placed him in the center of a circle of thinkers interested in theological and ecclesiastical criticism and renewal. The lecture, his commentary on Romans, and his newfound prominence in Germany all contributed to his appointment to the position of honorary professor of Reformed theology at the University of Göttingen in 1921. There he would begin his lifelong task of teaching and writing about the movement of God.

CHAPTER FOUR

The Impossible Possibility

The situation in Germany when Barth arrived in October 1921 was grim. The end of World War I was made official when the German government agreed to the terms of the Versailles Treaty in June 1919. While this treaty formally established peace in Europe, it was devastating for Germany and sowed the seeds for economic disaster and the emergence of Adolf Hitler and National Socialism in the 1930s. Germany was stripped of all its colonies, its military was reduced to a small fraction of what it had been, and the Rhineland was occupied by Allied troops to ensure permanent demilitarization. In addition, Germany had been forced to sign the "war guilt clause" in which it accepted sole responsibility for causing the war and thus was required to compensate the Allies for all of the losses and damages they had incurred in the conduct of the war, including pensions to Allied troops and all the costs of the occupation. These costs were well beyond the ability of the war-ravaged nation to pay, and initial installments on the debt were paid simply by printing more money, which drove inflation to staggering levels and made an already impossible economic situation even worse. Inevitably, Germany was unable to keep up with its financial obligations to the Allies, prompting further occupation and the seizure of factories and inventories, triggering a massive decline in the productivity of German industry and widespread unemployment. The hopelessness and despair of the German people was palpable, and riots became a common response to the desperate situation.

Politically, the situation was little better under the leadership of the ill-fated Weimar Republic. The republic, which came into being in the aftermath of the war and the demise of the monarchy, was conceived in the midst of defeat as a desperate measure to restore some sense of order after the havoc and devastation of the war. However, again and again it proved itself to be ineffective at the task of providing the leadership that was required in the face of the misery and suffering that shaped postwar German society. Over the course of its brief history it saw governments come and go as coalition after coalition proved to be unable to provide stable and effective leadership. The Weimar Republic, which had been born out of defeat and humiliation, was plagued by instability and turmoil and eventually ended in disaster as it gave way to the rise of National Socialism. Barth's time in Germany was set in the context of this transitional period in German history as the country struggled to regain its political and economic footing after the war.

Professor of Reformed Theology in Göttingen

Barth's move from Safenwil to Göttingen in the fall of 1921 to take up a university teaching position was a decisive event in the development of his life and his theology. It naturally provided him with a more prominent context from which to develop his thought—a university position in Germany as opposed to a small parish in Switzerland—and this would certainly increase his influence. However, the move to an academic setting also required a change in style and approach, if not substance, and Barth recognized this immediately. While he intended to articulate the same ideas that he had set forth in Safenwil, he realized that these had been more focused on criticism and the identification of errors and abuses, and that now he was "in the front rank" and had to take on responsibilities that he had not been aware of when he was, as he put it, "simply in opposition."[1] With his new position he had been given the

59

opportunity to work out his approach to theology in the fullest detail and to demonstrate its significance for the church and Christian witness. Barth was determined to make the most of this unexpected opportunity, and while he had not planned for it nor anticipated it, he certainly relished the challenges that it presented. However, he also realized at the outset that the work he was taking on entailed a breadth of knowledge which, by his own admission, he did not possess when he arrived in Göttingen, and that he would need to work feverishly to acquire it.

Barth's lack of knowledge extended to the area in which he was particularly commissioned to teach. As honorary professor of Reformed theology, he was to offer classes that introduced the Reformed confessions, expounded the teachings and insights of Reformed doctrine and theology, and gave due consideration to the life, ministry, and practices of Reformed churches. However, as he later admitted, in spite of his ministerial training and service in the Reformed church, when he began teaching at Göttingen he did not own a copy of the Reformed confessions nor had he even read them. Thus he labored long and hard, often burning the midnight oil in his efforts to understand and become thoroughly familiar with "the mysteries of specifically Reformed theology."[2] In order to prepare himself to teach Reformed dogmatics (more on the idea of dogmatics later), Barth followed the idea that the best way to learn something is to teach it and announced that he would lecture for several semesters on the theological history of the Reformed tradition, essentially for his own instruction. In his first five semesters he offered main lecture courses, generally consisting of three to four hours a week, on the Heidelberg Catechism (a standard outline of Reformed teaching presented in a question-and-answer format); the theology of John Calvin, the most important and seminal thinker in the Reformed tradition; the theology of the Swiss reformer and early Reformed theologian Huldrych Zwingli; the theology of the Reformed confessions; and finally the theology of Friedrich Schleiermacher. Through these lecture courses Barth was able to gain a detailed familiarity with the distinctive shape of Reformed theology in preparation for teaching dogmatics from a Reformed perspective. During these crucial semesters, he also offered shorter lecture courses, consisting of one hour per week, devoted to the theological interpretation of the New Testament.

In order to come to terms with the massive amount of material he needed to assimilate, Barth remembered that

he studied "night and day, going to and fro with books old and new until I had at least some skill in mounting the academic donkey (I could hardly call it a horse) and riding it to the university."[3] He often worked long into the night preparing for class, more than once finishing a lecture to be given early in the morning only a few hours prior to delivering it. Through this study, Barth became increasingly aware of the ways in which his emerging theology was consistent with the Reformed theological tradition. On one occasion he remarked, "Fortunately it turned out that my theology had become more Reformed, more Calvinistic than I had known, so I could pursue my special confessional task with delight and with a good conscience."[4]

However, Barth's growing appreciation for the theology of the tradition did not for a moment mean that he was uncritical of it. Indeed, in his first lectures on the Heidelberg Catechism he viewed it as a questionable work that represented a moment when the insights and ferment of the Reformation lapsed into theological complacency. He concluded that nothing of importance seemed to have occurred in the writing of the catechism. However, by the end of the semester he had shifted a bit, finding much to admire while still offering criticism. In the process of seeking to understand and come to terms with the emergence and history of Reformed theology, Barth increasingly came to see himself as being in remarkable relationship with the historical texts of the tradition, such that he was able to say that in one sense he could call everything good, while in another he believed everything was subject to critique. This sort of ongoing struggle and dialectical relationship with the ideas and doctrines of the sixteenth and seventeenth centuries was to shape the development of Barth's thinking at every turn as he sought to interpret the "orthodoxy" of Reformed Protestantism without simply reproducing its teachings in exactly the same way in which they were found in the texts of the tradition.

In this way Barth was giving expression to the idea that Reformed theology is reforming theology. This commitment, which arises from the Reformed concern for the ongoing reformation of the faith and practice of the church according to the Word of God in the context of ever-changing circumstances and situations, is captured in the saying "The reformed church is always reforming according to the Word of God." This concern for the continual reformation of the beliefs and practices of the church suggests a corresponding principle with respect to a Reformed understanding of theology. Reformed theology is always reforming according to the Word of God in order to bear witness to the gospel of Jesus Christ in the context of an ever-changing world characterized by a variety of cultural settings. One of the most central theological commitments that informs this approach to reformation and theology, the primacy and freedom of God in the governance and guidance of the church and the world, was already at the center of Barth's convictions concerning theology. Hence, the task of theology from a Reformed perspective is not, and never can be, something completed once and for all and appealed to in perpetuity as the "truly Reformed" position.

After his lectures on the Heidelberg Catechism, Barth turned his attention to the theology of John Calvin. Barth spoke of the experience of reading and lecturing on Calvin as an entirely new discovery that he likened to a mighty waterfall or a primitive forest, a strange and mythical power that surged straight down from the Himalayas, and one that absolutely overwhelmed his ability to absorb it or to make sense of it. He concluded that he could happily spend the rest of his life learning from Calvin, and he confessed that he could pass on to his students only a small sense of

what he had found and learned because he himself had so much yet to understand. Barth's critical appreciation of the Reformed confessional tradition and his intense fascination with Calvin shaped the development of his theology, and he became a more committed Reformed theologian who, in his words, "slowly but surely became intent on a pure *Reformed* theology."[5]

Since Barth was an honorary professor, students were not under any compulsion to attend his lectures, and initially the turnout was quite small. However, over the course of several semesters his lectures became increasingly well attended, in part because of the interest in Barth's emerging theology and also because he adopted the posture of a learner. He observed that the students were particularly interested in a professor who was also still a student and who continued to wrestle in fresh ways with theological questions. In turn, Barth thoroughly enjoyed his students and the openness and agility they brought to the task of theology. They became his partners in the early days of his new vocation as an academic theologian, and he found that they provided him with stimulation and considerable help through their remarks, protests, and objections to his research and teaching, which were beginning to blossom.

What he had craved in Safenwil, he now had in abundance in Göttingen, and he relished the opportunity to converse and debate matters with people in an intellectually stimulating environment. "I was more grateful than they could know for the gratitude which so many Göttingen students lavished on me."[6] At the conclusion of his first year of teaching, Barth delivered three special lectures that took his developing theology out of the lecture hall and made it available for pastors and theologians. Of particular importance was the third of these lectures, "The

Word of God as the Task of Theology" (translated as "The Word of God and the Task of Ministry" in the collection of essays that make up the book *The Word of God and the Word of Man,* from which citations will be made), delivered in Elgersburg, in which Barth provided a detailed and programmatic reflection on his approach to theological method for the first time.

The Impossible Possibility of Theology

In this address Barth takes up the thesis that was cited in the last chapter concerning dialectical theology, "As ministers [or, theologians] we ought to speak of God. We are human, however, and so cannot speak of God. We ought therefore to recognize both *our obligation and our inability* and by that very recognition give God the glory."[7] These three assertions provide the structure of the lecture, and Barth devotes a section of the address to each of them in turn. In the second of these sections, which considers the inability of human beings to speak of God, he takes up a consideration of method. He considers three ways in which theologians have sought to speak about God over the course of history: the dogmatic way, the self-critical way, and the dialectical way. The dogmatic approach is the way of traditional orthodoxy, which tends to assume that the relationship between God and its theological assertions about God is essentially direct, that its statements about God correspond with the objective reality of God. The problem here is that the living reality of God, as the one who is infinite, eternal, and transcendent, is in fact negated by the "taste for objectivity" that characterizes the dogmatic approach. This way fails in the end because it substitutes its statements and assertions *about* God for the Word *of* God, the divine speech, apart from which theology can-

not fulfill its appointed tasks. The dogmatic way ultimately fails because, like all human ways, it cannot speak of God. The debilitating weakness of the dogmatic approach is that it does not recognize this inability.

The self-critical approach is the way of mysticism and idealism, which seeks to speak of God by the negation of humanity. In this approach, "God is not this or that; he is no object, no something, no opposite, no second; he is pure being, without quality, filling everything, obstructed only by the particular individuality of man. Let this latter finally be removed and the soul will of a certainty conceive God."[8] Barth refers to this as self-criticism because it calls on humans to decrease and place themselves under judgment, to acknowledge their limitations and inability. This self-critical, mystical approach is strongest where the dogmatic is weakest and yet still comes up short. "Here something happens; here we are not left standing with instructions to believe; here we are seriously attacked. . . . But even here we cannot speak of God."[9] What is certain in this way is that humanity must be negated. Yet what must be remembered is that no negation that human beings are capable of attaining is as all-encompassing and fundamental as the ultimate Negation brought about by the power and true presence of God.

The dialectical approach is, according to Barth, the best by far, and he associates it with Paul and the Reformers. The truths contained in the dogmatic and self-critical approaches are presupposed by it, but with an awareness of their fragmentary and relative nature. "This way from the outset undertakes seriously and positively to develop the idea of God on the one hand and the criticism of man and all things human on the other; but they are not now considered independently but are both referred constantly to their common presupposition, to the living truth which, to be sure, may not be named, but which lies between them and gives to both their meaning and interpretation."[10] However, even in the dialectical approach, it is still the case that human beings are not able to speak of God since they are incapable of relating the affirmations of the dogmatic approach or the negations of the self-critical approach to the reality of the living God at the center of theology, since God never enters into the control of human beings. Therefore the only thing that properly can be done is to bear witness to the realities of this situation and to take care to continually relate human affirmations and human negations to each other.

The genuine dialectician knows that this living center cannot be apprehended or beheld and will therefore give direct information and communication about it as seldom as possible in the knowledge "that all such information, whether it be positive or negative, is *not* really information, but always *either* dogma *or* self-criticism. On this narrow ridge of rock one can only walk." If we attempt to stand

still, we will fall to either the right or the left; hence, the only choice is to keep moving forward, constantly looking from one side to the other, from positive to negative and from negative to positive.[11] Each of the approaches Barth mentions contains elements of truth. The dialectical is preferable because it attempts to relate the insights of the dogmatic and self-critical approaches, but not because it is more successful than these ways. The fundamental assertion remains; we cannot speak of God. From the standpoint of human beings, theology is an impossibility. Theology becomes possible only where God speaks when God is spoken of. Since human beings have no control over this self-revelatory speech, they are *always* dependent on God in the task of theology.

Given the reality of this state of affairs, what humans are able to do is bear witness to their creaturely inadequacy by the continual negation of theological assertions through the affirmation of alternative and opposing assertions. This ongoing practice of setting statement against statement constitutes the shape of Barth's dialectical theological method. But this dialectical method *is not* the means by which humans are able to speak of God. It is, rather, an emergency measure adopted as the only possible way to bear witness to the impossibility of human speech about God in light of their obligation to bear witness. Further, Barth notes that whenever the dialectical method has appeared to make human language significant and capable of bearing witness to the reality of the living God, it is important to remember that this was not achieved because of what the dialectician did or because of the dialectical assertions that were made. Rather, it is because the living truth at the center of ultimate reality, the reality of God, was asserted by God in accordance with the freedom and will of God and God alone. "But this possibility, the possibility that God *himself* speaks when he is spoken of, is not part of the dialectic way as such; it arises rather at the point where this way *comes to an end*."[12]

In other words, since the goal of theology is to speak the Word of God in the way that God would speak it, theology is not humanly possible, because this standard is unattainable for humans and no method can ever make it so. However, this does not mean that theology is utterly impossible; it simply means that where it is possible, it is so only as a divine possibility. Only by the grace of God in which God takes up human words and uses them for the purposes of self-revelation, in spite of their inherent inadequacy, does theology become possible. Hence, theology is an impossible possibility that is made possible only by the will of God. The dialectical method serves as the means of bearing formal witness to the inadequacy of human beings for the task of theology and their dependence on God.

Two years later Barth would, for the first time, lecture on Christian dogmatics and begin his lifelong project of

giving detailed theological expression to these seminal ideas.

Göttingen Dogmatics

Early in 1924 Barth turned his attention to the task of lecturing on dogmatics for the first time in the summer semester. Dogmatics refers to the attempt to clarify the distinctive content of the Christian faith for the church in order to enable the Christian community to be clear about what it believes in its witness to the world. It is also an investigation of the content of Christian theology for the practical purpose of considering how that content is to be most properly and effectively conveyed and communicated in each new social, linguistic, and cultural setting. In this sense, as Barth himself was later to say, "dogmatics as such does not ask what the apostles and prophets said but what we must say on the basis of the apostles and prophets."[13]

Barth was intent on developing an account of dogmatics in line with his convictions concerning the impossible possibility of theology and the formal principles of the dialectical method he had articulated in the Elgersburg lecture as well as the perspectives he had set forth in his Romans commentary and the Tambach lecture. However, as he faced the challenge of moving from the critique of a dominant theological position and the articulation of some formal principles to the full-scale construction of a new model, he was plagued with doubt. "I shall never forget the spring vacation of 1924. I sat in my study at Göttingen, faced with the task of giving lectures on dogmatics for the first time. No one can ever have been more plagued than I was then with the problem, could I do it? and how?" He was further aware that his recent efforts in biblical and historical studies had "more and more expelled me from the goodly society of contemporary, and, as I began to realize ever more clearly, of almost the whole of the more recent theology; and I saw myself, as it were, alone in the open without a teacher."[14]

Barth's "discovery" of the strange new world within the Bible and his subsequent engagement with it in teaching and preaching had convinced him that Scripture must be the controlling element in his dogmatics. He was also committed to connecting his work with that of the Protestant Reformers, and particularly with the Reformed tradition. The question was how to do it in the midst of the various options. He observed regarding his commitment to the Bible that he "was more terrified of the footprints of modern Biblicism than attracted to them." He also realized that his desire to connect with the Reformers was hardly unique; after all, as he put it, "What soul in the last two centuries of Protestant theological history had not meant to hitch everything on to the Reformers? What was the effect of that on Protestant dogmatics? What could I see happening right and left of me, over and over again?" Much to his surprise, Barth found help from an unexpected source, the recently published *Reformed Dogmatics* by Heinrich Heppe, a collection of texts from Reformed theologians dating from the sixteenth century to the early eighteenth that covered all of the standard topics of dogmatics. He described the volume as being "out of date, dusty, unattractive, almost like a table of logarithms, dreary to read, stiff and eccentric on almost every page I opened."[15]

In spite of his initial impressions, Barth persevered and soon discovered that he had entered an "atmosphere in which the road by way of the Reformers to H[oly] Scripture was a more sensible and natural one to tread, than the atmosphere, now only too familiar to me, of the theological literature determined by Schleiermacher and Ritschl."[16] This discovery of Reformed orthodoxy, the period following the first two generations of reformers such as Zwingli and Calvin in which their insights were codified and shaped into grand systems of theology, was immensely important to Barth. Indeed, the influence of the Reformed theologians is evident throughout his first lectures on dogmatics, and they had a significant impact on the shape and development of his thought. He cites them frequently, more frequently in

fact than either Luther or Calvin, and engages them with the utmost seriousness, in keeping with his positive assessment of their theological perceptivity and powers of explication and description.

Barth was deeply impressed by the discipline and depth of treatment that these thinkers brought to the work of theology, and longed to possess something of "the same remarkable objectivity and perspicacity" that characterized "the masters of the old theological school" in their engagement with theological ideas and questions.[17] The strong interest and respect that Barth felt toward these theologians was particularly connected to the manifestly ecclesial character of their thought. They displayed dogmatics as a discipline in service to the church, and this insight would exercise a significant influence on Barth throughout his work. In light of his appreciation for "the older dogmaticians," Barth urged his students to regard the compendiums of the Lutheran and Reformed scholastic theology as crucial background material for the work of contemporary dogmatics and to read them before turning their attention to the literature of Schleiermacher and modern theology.

Two points should be noted with respect to Barth's use of the sources of Reformed orthodoxy. First, in spite of his appreciation for them, it was also clear to him that a simple return to the conclusions and assertions of these writers was not an option, and he frequently offered sharp critiques of their positions. While it was important to Barth to maintain continuity with this tradition, he also maintained that this could not involve simply a "repristination of the older Christian or Reformed dogmatics."[18] This is because true dogma is something to be sought, not given. Received dogmas or theological doctrines, while important, are still in principle "changeable, reformable, and in need of supplementation."[19] As such, they serve as preliminary stopping points in the ongoing task of theological reflection in the church that must be examined, scrutinized, and tested again and again in order to see if they can be reestablished or if they are in need of correction.

Second, Barth's use and deployment of these sources serve as a reminder of his positive and constructive concerns in the task of dogmatics. This is important to bear in mind in the context of the more critical posture adopted in many of Barth's earlier writings, which were particularly concerned with the stringent critique of liberalism and its cavalier and domesticated assumptions about the general availability of the knowledge of God for human beings. To this idea Barth offers a resounding "No!" But this should not detract from, nor draw our attention away from, the

Yes that is under and above the No by the grace and will of God. Barth was never simply a critical thinker who was bereft of concern for the positive affirmations of a theology of the Word of God. The predominance of criticism in his earliest writings was due to his perception of the fundamental distortions that had been introduced not only into the discipline of theology, but into the broader Christian culture, and the corresponding eclipse of the language and thought of the classical Christian tradition. Hence, he found that he had to say "no" long and loud in order to create space for positive affirmations. "The devastating negation under which we live has its positive, obverse side."[20] In other words, ground clearing and construction were going on together all the time, even if the ground clearing was more predominant in the early part of

Barth's career. After all, in a construction project the ground must be cleared and prepared before full-scale building can take place, and if the initial phase of a project is more destructive, it is also true that the constructive intent is always in view.

We will consider the content of Barth's mature dogmatics in chapter 6 and so will not examine this first cycle of lectures except to note their great theme that God is God. Early on and throughout his transition and pilgrimage from liberalism, Barth had expressed the concern that whatever was to be done in theology, it was of the greatest importance to begin at the beginning and recognize that God is God. This means that God is the living and free Lord of all creation and that all we think and say about this God must bear witness that we are human and not God. God and humanity are categorically different, Creator and creature, and must never be confused, but it is also true that in freedom God is able to establish genuine communion with humanity and put the Word of God "in our hearts and on our lips."[21] That God is God means that the relationship between God and human beings is never characterized by symmetry, but is always asymmetrical. God always has the initiative and the priority, while human beings are always in a position of dependence on God. It means that while theology is an impossibility for human beings, it is an impossibility that becomes possible in the freedom of God at the instigation of God. We are human and not God. God is God.

The assertion that God is God also carries profound political and cultural entailments. It means that all rivals, symbols, and pretensions that set themselves up against the knowledge of God must stand down, for the knowledge and reality of God means "the most radical twilight of the gods. Olympus and Valhalla are emptied out and become secular. Their inhabitants become successively weaker as ideas, demons, ghosts, and finally comic figures. . . . There is only one God. No statement is more dangerous or revolutionary than this for all mythologies and ideologies."[22] This conviction would eventually place Barth in direct conflict with one of the most infamous claimants of God's position in the twentieth century as the political situation in Germany moved inexorably toward the rise of National Socialism.

CHAPTER FIVE

Bearing Christian Witness

Professor at Münster

After four years in Göttingen, Barth was appointed as professor of dogmatics and New Testament exegesis at the University of Münster in July of 1925. He arrived in Münster in late October and took up his new position on the relatively small Protestant theological faculty at the university. While Göttingen had been a stronghold of Lutheranism, Münster was a predominantly Catholic city. This change of venue and context was symbolic in that Barth was growing increasingly interested in conversation and debate with the Roman Catholic theological tradition. More and more he was coming to view ongoing discussion with liberal Protestantism as something of a dead end.

While neo-Protestants were focused primarily on the philosophy of religion and the study of history, Barth had a burning interest in the kinds of theological issues and questions that had been left behind and forgotten in the advent of liberal theology. In Catholic theologians he discovered dialogue partners who, while differing with him substantially on many points of interpretation, shared his intense interest in material theological questions.

In the light of this discovery, Barth devoted increasing attention to Catholic theology during his years at Münster, seeking to explain the ways in which he found Catholicism attractive, particularly over against liberal Protestantism, as well as the places where he felt compelled to offer vigorous criticism. Barth asserted that when Catholics and Protestants spoke of the church they were speaking of the same reality, but also that each of them spoke of this reality in quite different and theologically incompatible ways. Each of these assertions is important. Concerning the first, Barth maintained that conversation between Catholics and Protestants could not be pursued on the assumption that the other side was in fact engaged in a form of idolatry. This would make the conversation all too easy, if not pleasant, and suggest that the division between the two was not painful or in need of healing. If such were the case, each side could simply issue an appropriate condemnation and move on. However, such was not the case; the pain of the division was genuine and palpable and served to invoke ongoing conversation. The content of this shared reality concerning the church is seen in the common speech and mutual confession of each side: the church is one, holy, catholic, and apostolic.

However, having affirmed this reality, Barth also notes the decisive difference between Catholics and Protestants concerning the way in which this common reality is understood. This decisive difference is centered on the nature of grace. For the Catholic Church, grace is made available through the agency and mediation of the historical, institutional church founded by the apostles and centered in Rome. The church is entrusted and empowered by God to communicate grace through the presence, ministry, and sacraments of the Roman Catholic Church in accordance with the Catholic understanding of Scripture and tradition. In this context, the notion of apostolic succession is crucial to the integrity of the Catholic Church in the fulfilling of its divine mandate. For Protestants, the central conviction concerning the nature of grace is that the church does not possess the slightest mastery or control over grace. While the church is the instrument of God's grace in the world as a visible and historical institution, this does not in any way imply that the church has any control over the dispensation of grace in the world. This prerogative belongs to God and

to God alone. Grace constitutes God's claim on humanity, and this understanding cannot be reversed, or grace becomes something that enters into human control and as such is no longer grace. Hence, neither the church nor any individuals in the church have a claim on the grace of God.

"The splendour of the church can consist only in its hearing in poverty the Word of the eternally rich God, and making that Word heard by [human beings]. The Church does not control that Word as earthly things can be controlled. Nor does the church possess the Word as material or intellectual goods are normally possessed. Nor does the Church take the Word for granted as it would count on something which was not a gift."[1] Thus, from Barth's perspective, the four marks of unity, holiness, catholicity, and apostolicity are not given to the church such that they become part of its constituent nature. Instead, they are always to be understood as properties of God's action by which he brings the church into existence moment by moment.

In his engagement with Catholicism, Barth makes it quite clear that he takes the tradition with the seriousness of a highly esteemed and valued conversation partner. Although the language employed is quite strong on many occasions, it must always be remembered that for Barth, vigorous and passionate debate over differences, so often viewed with scorn in our culture, constitutes a sign of deepest respect rather than derision and contempt. It means an acknowledgment that the other has something worth listening to with care and attention. Indeed, Barth came to regard the Catholic tradition as being closer to the thought and spirit of the Reformers than was the liberal Protestantism that claimed the heritage of the Reformation. He states of the Catholic Church that "in spite of all contradictions, it is closer to the Reformers than is the

Church of the Reformation so far as that has actually and finally become the new Protestantism."[2]

Barth's stance with respect to the Catholic tradition earned him considerable respect among Catholic theologians over the course of his career, and he assumed the role of a leading Protestant statesman in the dialogue with Catholicism. One of the most important Catholic theologians of the twentieth century, Hans Urs von Balthasar, noted the significance of Barth as a Catholic conversation partner with the following words: "We have in Barth, then, two crucial features: the most thorough and penetrating display of the Protestant view and the closest rapprochement with the Catholic . . . we have the fullest and most systematic working out of the contrasts that distinguish Protestant from Catholic views."[3]

While at Münster, Barth also offered his second cycle of lectures on dogmatics. The first volume of a projected three-volume series on these lectures was published in

1927, but the series was discontinued after Barth became unsatisfied with what he had written, convinced that he still needed further clarification concerning his theological method and the overall shape of the dogmatics he wanted to write. Hence, he found himself ready to "begin again at the beginning" in his efforts to produce a dogmatics that bore proper witness to the living God. Then, on October 26, 1929, Barth was appointed to the chair of systematic theology on the Protestant theological faculty at Bonn. He spent one more semester in Münster, serving as dean of the faculty, before moving to Bonn in March 1930 to begin teaching there in the second semester.

Teaching at Bonn

Barth's appointment at Bonn changed the fortunes of the theological faculty dramatically. The number of students doubled immediately and continued to grow, to a peak of about four hundred, until the political situation changed the landscape. Barth's main lecture courses were held in one of the largest lecture halls in the university, which seated more than three hundred students. Barth's lectures became so popular that he regularly filled the room to capacity. Nearly all of the theology students attended his lectures. Likewise, his seminars were in such high demand that he was forced to limit participation to thirty students, while allowing for another thirty auditors. Barth administered an exam to determine who was able to participate. When compared to the situation at Göttingen, where he struggled to attract students, it was clear that Barth had arrived as a teacher whose ideas were of increasing fascination and interest. Students packed his classes, eager to hear the development of his theology.

In the summer semester of 1931, Barth set off on his

third lecture cycle on dogmatics. This cycle would occupy him for the rest of his career and come to be published as his magnum opus, *Church Dogmatics*. In these lectures, Barth began the process of forging a full-scale constructive account of dogmatics that built on the critical insights of his early career and sought to maintain a theological position in which God is God. In so doing he changed the face of theology in the twentieth century. The next chapter will provide a brief overview of this important work. One important point to note here, however, is the change in nomenclature from "Christian" dogmatics to "church" dogmatics.

Barth had long expressed concern for what he perceived to be the tendency toward triumphalism in the church,

85

which he viewed as being connected with the all-too-common tendency in theology to confuse the Holy Spirit and the human spirit, particularly in the liberal tradition. He suggested that in order to avoid this, it would be good to be more cautious in the use of the word "Christian" than had become customary in the contemporary church. What do we mean when we speak of a Christian worldview, a Christian society, Christian ethics, Christian art, and Christian institutions? Such cavalier speech fails to recognize that the legitimate use of the adjective "Christian" in its most true and genuine sense lies completely beyond the ability and authority of human beings. Along these lines, Barth remarks in the preface to the first volume of the *Church Dogmatics* that in "substituting the word Church for Christian in the title, I have tried to set a good example of restraint in the lighthearted use of the great word 'Christian' against which I have protested." This change also pointed to the fact that the task of dogmatics "is not a free science. It is bound to the sphere of the Church, where alone it is possible and meaningful."[4] This change thus represented yet another move away from liberal Protestantism and its incessant preoccupation with the individual.

Barth's move to Bonn coincided with changing political fortunes in Germany and the ominous rise of the National Socialist Party. Skyrocketing unemployment in Germany coupled with the global effects of the stock market crash of 1929 created a state of economic depression and political crisis. An emergency powers provision in the Weimar constitution was invoked that gave the president the right to make government policy by decree. In this context the Communists and the National Socialists gained significant numbers of seats in the parliament. The National Socialists resorted to brutal tactics and helped to render the parliament completely dysfunctional. This caused the political

situation to spin out of control and effectively ended the Weimar Republic. The collapse of interim government after interim government eventually resulted in the appointment of Adolf Hitler as chancellor in January 1933. A month later the Reichstag was burned down, almost certainly by Hitler's supporters, but the arson was blamed on the Communists. A state of emergency was declared and Hitler was appointed dictator on March 23, 1933, after which competing political parties were banned and their members were arrested or forced to flee. Within a short period of time the National Socialists were the only political party in Germany and Hitler was in complete control of the government, with devastating consequences for his political opponents and for the Jewish citizens of Germany, who began to be persecuted and arrested immediately after Hitler's assumption of power.

Like much of Germany, Barth was slow to recognize the extreme danger posed by the Nazis, but by 1931 Barth was able to see that the German political situation was "like sitting in a car which is driven by a man who is either incompetent or drunk."[5] In May of 1931 he joined the Social Democrat Party in protest against the growing threat to democracy. He did this after ten years in Germany without any particular political affiliation, observing that in view of the impending fascist terror, it was good to make it clear with whom he would like to be imprisoned and hanged. In 1933 he was asserting that one was not preaching the gospel of Jesus Christ in Germany during this time if that proclamation was not coupled with a stand against the disappearance and persecution of the Jews. This stance led Barth into direct opposition with Hitler and the Nazi party.

Opposing Hitler

To say that Barth, along with other Christians, opposed Hitler might appear to be stating the obvious. After all, from what we know from history concerning the activities of Hitler and the Nazi party, we would like to believe that the church would have opposed Hitler, even if the larger German population had been seduced into following him by the promise of economic recovery and political stability. Sadly, this was not the case, in part because of the liberal, cultural Protestantism that Barth had been revolting against. In spite of what we might like to assume, support for Hitler extended into the church. Part of what made the German church susceptible to the emergence of a leader like Hitler was the way in which it had been affected by a strongly nationalistic ideology that found much popular

support among the German people due to the perceived injustice of the Versailles Treaty that had officially ended World War I. This was particularly problematic for the Protestant churches in Germany, and most especially the Lutherans, whose origins were deeply bound up with the emergence and rise of a national German identity. In the popular German mind, Martin Luther was not simply a Protestant church reformer but also a national hero. Right-wing nationalists like the Nazi party, as well as others, made use of Luther's iconic status and co-opted his legacy in support of their own agenda.

The notion of a church that would give specific expression to the particularly German soul and mind was not new, and was increasingly common by 1930. As the political power of the Nazi party grew in the early 1930s, so did a group of fervent supporters in the Protestant and Catholic churches who were known as the German Christians. The German Christians were inspired by earlier ecclesial movements that asserted such ideas as the superiority of the German people, need for racial purity, and intense opposition to Communists, Jews, and others who did not share their beliefs. Further, these ideas were not limited to the more populist, rank-and-file sphere of the culture, but were also strongly proclaimed and defended by many of the leading intellectuals in German universities, such as theologians Friedrich Gogarten and Paul Althaus, church historians Reinhold Seeberg and Emanuel Hirsch, and philosopher Martin Heidegger. The German Christians were officially organized in June 1932 and supported the National Socialists through the founding of a newspaper and other public events.

Hitler knew that the Catholic and Protestant churches made up an enormously important part of German life and he needed to deal with them carefully, but decisively. He reached a concordat with the Catholic Church but realized that Protestant churches would be more difficult to deal with, since they lacked a central authority. To address this challenge, Hitler proposed the formation of an Evangelical (or Protestant) Reich Church and appointed Ludwig Müller to oversee its affairs. In a nationwide radio address he demanded that the church support the state while guaranteeing "inner freedom" concerning religious life. However, as soon as the Nazis' control of the churches was secure, they began to intervene coercively in the life of the church in order to remake it in the image of National

Socialism. Perhaps the most egregious example of this intervention was the adoption of the so-called Aryan paragraph, which stated that neither non-Aryans nor those married to non-Aryans could be employed by the church. It also called for the exclusion from the church of all Christians with Jewish ancestry.

In response to the emergence of the German Christian movement and the intrusions of the National Socialists in the life of the church, an opposition movement emerged that called for a free and confessing church. Martin Niemöller organized the Pastors' Emergency League, a resistance effort that attracted a large following among church leaders. In 1932, shortly before Hitler's rise to full power, the Altona declaration was issued in response to the events known as Bloody Sunday, when the Nazis took to the streets of Altona and ruthlessly quashed opposition to

Hitler in the name of law and order. It declared that when governing authorities ignore their mandate to seek and promote the good of civil society, then Christians must choose to obey God rather than these human authorities. Other protests included the Düsseldorf Theses set forth by Reformed theologians, including Karl Barth; the Bethel Confession, which included a paragraph drafted by Dietrich Bonhoeffer against the infamous Aryan paragraph; and a Confession of Faith from the Synod of Biefeld following the Nazi seizure of the headquarters of the German Evangelical Church.

Karl Barth directly opposed Hitler and the Nazis himself when he traveled to Berlin to deliver an address titled "The Reformation as Decision" at the Reformation festival on October 30. In spite of the fact that the lecture was not advertised, the hall was packed to hear Barth declare that the Reformation should be seen as the decision to recognize the rule of God as absolute. At various times other alternatives to faith and trust in God present themselves, such as forms of morality, culture, reason, experience, and tradition. In the present situation the leading alternative was the Nazi state. Allowing any of these to encroach on faith and the absolute rule of God constitutes disloyalty to the spirit of the Reformation and the fundamental Reformation decision. Fortified by this Reformation decision, those who had not already succumbed to the National Socialists had no choice but to offer resistance. At the mention of resistance, a burst of spontaneous and thundering applause broke out for several minutes. On the resumption of his address, Barth told an old Swiss story of resistance to the Austrian army, when one of the Swiss soldiers had called out in encouragement, "Smite their spears, for they are hollow!" Barth went on to say that in the light of the rule of God, the spears and threats of the National Socialists "*are* hollow." This story from Barth's rousing address in Berlin became a watchword for the Confessing Church.[6]

The Barmen Declaration

It was in the context of these events that the Confessing Church called for a national synod of the German churches to be held in Barmen to reiterate their common faith in the gospel of Jesus Christ and declare that this faith compelled their resistance to Hitler and to the imposition of his National Socialist agenda on the church in Germany. In preparation for the meeting in Barmen, a theological committee was appointed by the leaders of the Confessing Church to write the theological theses for the synod. On May 16, Barth, representing the Reformed Church, met with two representatives from the Lutheran Church at a hotel in Frankfurt to draft what came to be known as the

Barmen Declaration. Barth described the scene by recalling that the "Lutheran Church slept and the Reformed Church kept awake," meaning that while the two Lutheran theologians had a lengthy nap, Barth, "fortified by strong coffee and one or two Brazilian cigars," revised the text of the six statements, resulting in a finished text by the evening. Concerning his authorship, Barth humbly stated, "I don't want to boast, but it really was my text."[7]

From May 29 to 31, 1934, delegates from all over Germany took part in the first Confessing Synod of the German Evangelical Church. Although Barth was the chief author of the declaration, he did not speak publicly, instead working behind the scenes as part of the theological commission until the declaration was approved on May 31. The heart of the declaration is found in the six theses set forth in part 2. Each of the theses sets forth one or more quotations of Scripture in order to bear witness to the principle that church confessions or declarations are to be understood as an explication and application of Scripture in a particular context. In addition, each of the affirmations of the declaration is followed by corresponding denials to affirm that the "yes" of God in the gospel entails a necessary "no" to beliefs and practices that are contrary to Christian faith and life.

The first thesis sets the tone for the rest of the document with its straightforward affirmation: "Jesus Christ, as he is testified to us in the Holy Scripture, is the one Word of God, whom we are to hear, whom we are to trust and obey in life and death." Of the denials, two that particularly strike at the Nazi regime will be mentioned here: "We repudiate the false teaching that the Church can and may, apart from [its] ministry, set up special leaders [*Führer*] equipped with powers to rule"; and "We repudiate the false teaching that the state can and should expand beyond its

special responsibility to become the single and total order of human life" and that the "church can and should expand beyond its special responsibility to take the characteristics, functions and dignities of the state, and thereby become itself an organ of the state."[8]

In order to appreciate the significance of the Barmen declaration and its stance against Hitler and the Nazi regime, it is important to remember that opposing the Nazis was not popular among the German people in 1934. Many considered such opposition to be something ranging from unpatriotic to treasonous. Hence, what seems so clear and courageous from the perspective of history was hardly self-evident at the time from the perspective of German popular opinion. For all of the strength of Barmen, however, there was one thing that Barth later described as a failing: he had not made the Jewish question a decisive feature in his draft of the document. Later he commented:

"Of course, in 1934 no text in which I had done that would have been acceptable even to the Confessing Church, given the atmosphere that there was then. But that does not excuse me for not having at least gone through the motions of fighting."[9]

Barth's opposition to National Socialism, his principal role in the authorship of the Barmen declaration, and his stance on the Jewish question—that if people were not preaching specifically against the persecution and disappearance of the Jews, then they were not preaching the gospel, no matter what else they might say—all led to his refusal to give an unqualified oath of loyalty to Adolf Hitler in the required form on November 7, 1934. Hitler announced that the oath would be required after he had combined the offices of chancellor and president and had taken them over himself. When Barth heard the news, he realized that he would not be able to take the oath in the prescribed form. When he was ordered to do so by the rector of the university, he made a proposal to be passed on to the appropriate officials: "I did not refuse to give the offi-

cial oath, but I stipulated an addition to the effect that I could be loyal to the Führer only within my responsibilities as an Evangelical Christian."[10] His proposal was summarily rejected and he was suspended from his teaching duties at Bonn on November 26. On June 22, 1935, he was formally dismissed from his position by the minister of cultural affairs in Berlin. Within three days of the announcement of his dismissal from Bonn, he was offered a chair in theology at the University of Basel, which he immediately accepted, bringing his years of teaching in Germany to an end.

CHAPTER SIX

Church Dogmatics

In July of 1935, Karl Barth and his family arrived in Basel, the city of his birth, where he took up the chair in theology that he would hold at the university until his retirement from teaching in 1962. Over the course of this time, Barth lived an immeasurably rich life filled with conversation and consultation with many friends and important thinkers, secure in the knowledge that he was the leading Protestant theologian in Europe. Students traveled from all over the world to attend his lectures and seminars and sit under his tutelage. During the years in Germany he had found his theological voice, and in Basel he continued the process of honing his thoughts and bringing them to fruitful maturity. Among the numerous works he published during these years, the most significant and enduring are his four volumes of the *Church Dogmatics*. This chapter will summarize some of the main ideas and themes in this monumental work. No brief and basic summary can even begin to do adequate justice to a work so vast in scope and rich in complexity. What we will seek to do is provide a very basic orientation tour that is intended to both stimulate an interest in actually reading the *Dogmatics* and help would-be readers to get started.

Faith Seeking Understanding

In the *Church Dogmatics*, Barth developed a form of theological discourse that was counter-intuitive to the assumptions of the time. In order to appreciate this development, it will help to reflect a bit further on the significance of Barth's conception of his project as "church" dogmatics. In short, from Barth's perspective, dogmatics were to be most properly written from the church, to the church, and for the church. In this way, Barth's work is considerably different from the standard apologetic approach to modern theology that is constantly concerned with the task of critically establishing and defending the possibility of Christian belief. In contrast to the apologetic or foundationalist approach, Barth's interest is not with the possibility of faith or the church, but rather with providing a description of theology from the perspective of the Christian church. In other words, instead of investing energy in trying to demonstrate or prove the viability and truth of Christian belief, Barth assumes it and then seeks to describe it. He thus challenged the long-standing assumptions of modern theology that the rationality of Christian faith was suspect or untenable and hence needed to derive its basic concepts from other disciplines, such as history or philosophy.

From Barth's perspective, theology could recover its essential integrity only when it came to realize that it was utterly dependent on God's self-revelation in Jesus Christ, which constituted its only possible basis. Dependence on revelation means that we cannot assume that we know in advance what reality and the nature of rationality look like and then assess revelation and Christian faith by these pre-determined standards. Instead we must begin with faith in Jesus Christ and only then attempt to explain the internal rationality and intelligibility of such faith. In short, we must first believe and then try to understand what we believe. While this approach, known as faith seeking understanding, had been largely dismissed in modern theology, it had an impressive pedigree in the classical Christian tradition. Barth's own work had been moving steadily in this direction throughout his academic career, but he identified his study of the medieval theologian Anselm early in his tenure at Bonn as being of particular importance in helping to solid-ify this approach in his mind. What Barth saw in Anselm was a theology that moved *from* the confession of the church concerning God *to* theological understanding.

In a book on Anselm's understanding of God, Barth observes that Anselm does not attempt to make God and Christian faith more plausible to his readers through various interpretive strategies, nor does he make understanding God a requirement for faith. Instead, he prays patiently for the wisdom he requires in order to understand something of God's being and majesty. On this model we do not assume that we possess the truth about God in advance of our investigation or even that our investigations and discourse will be adequate for the task of seeking to understand God. In fact, we know that they will not, but we pray that in the act of our seeking and investigation and through our finite words and limited comprehension, God will be made known.

Barth's study of Anselm[1] provides a particularly helpful articulation of the approach to theology that shapes the *Church Dogmatics*. In fact, the Anselm book can be read helpfully in conjunction with it as a formal statement of what the *Dogmatics* is seeking to accomplish. This approach implies a more dogmatic method, in which the basis for theological reflection and investigation is to be found in the life and faith of the Christian community. This means that for Barth the work of theology or dogmatics takes the form of ongoing and extended grappling with the questions raised by Christian faith and witness and their implications for belief and practice, based on a constant, careful, and attentive listening to Scripture. In other words, theology, in Barth's account, is scriptural reasoning in conversation with the Christian tradition in its various cultural settings. However, this should not be taken to mean that Barth ever ceased to be a dialectical theologian, merely that his conception and articulation of dialectical theology found its starting point in the church. As a result of the evolution of his thinking over the years in the direction of faith seeking understanding, coupled with his extensive and intensive work in biblical exegesis and his increasing knowledge of the classical tradition of the church, he had found the freedom to think and write confessionally from the standpoint of the church without becoming anxious about the task of securing extratheological starting points outside of the Christian faith in order to establish the possibility of theology. As Barth himself observed of his emergence in the writing of the *Dogmatics*: "I can say everything far more clearly, unambiguously, simply, and more in the way of a confession, and at the same time also much more freely, openly, and comprehensively, than I could ever say it before."[2]

The Shape of the *Church Dogmatics*

Barth planned that his *Church Dogmatics* would be unfolded in five volumes, one for each of the major doctrines of the faith: revelation or the Word of God, God, creation, reconciliation, and redemption. Because of the length of Barth's exposition, each volume contains multiple part-volumes. Volume 1, on the doctrine of the Word of God, contains two part-volumes (I/1–2); volume 2 concerns the doctrine of God and also consists of two part-volumes (II/1–2); volume 3 deals with the doctrine of creation and has four part-volumes (III/1–4); and volume 4, on the doctrine of reconciliation, consists of four part-volumes (IV/1–4), with the third part-volume divided into two halves and the fourth consisting of a shorter fragment. Barth did not live to write the fifth volume, on redemption, nor was he able to complete the nearly finished volume on reconciliation. In all, the *Dogmatics* consists of thirteen separate books and nearly eight thousand pages of material in the English translation.

Each volume is divided not only into chapters, as one would expect, but also into "paragraphs." However, these paragraphs are not what we normally mean when we use the word to describe a relatively short portion of material in the context of a much larger composition. In the *Dogmatics* a paragraph refers to a self-contained section of the work that addresses a particular topic. These sections of material vary greatly in length and are sometimes fairly short, consisting of about fifty pages or so, but they can go on at considerable length. The paragraphs are an especially important device for following the main flow of the discussion, and Barth provides a thesis to introduce each new section of material. The paragraphs are further divided into

subsections. Hence, chapter 1 of the *Church Dogmatics*, "The Word of God as the Criterion of Dogmatics," is divided into five paragraphs and seventeen subsections. As a whole the *Dogmatics* consists of sixteen chapters and seventy-three paragraphs plus the fragment that makes up IV/4. Taking careful note of these divisions and the transitions that they represent in the development of the work will be of considerable help in discerning the general shape of such a long and detailed presentation and tracking its direction.

One of the particularly interesting features of this work that confronts readers immediately on opening any of the volumes is the presence of passages in small print that can range in length from a few lines to fifty pages. These are known as excursus and are supplemental to the main argument, though not at all unimportant. They sometimes function as footnotes, providing information concerning sources or offering a brief comment on Barth's general exposition or a particular argument. But they are also where he engages in detailed biblical exegesis and carries on conversations with other thinkers and theologians throughout the history of the church. They are a rich resource in their own right and provide an opportunity to "think along" with Barth and follow the detailed analysis of particular texts, thinkers, and developments that have shaped his thinking in the formation and expansion of his argument. First-time readers can skip this material if they wish without losing track of the flow of thought, since the main text contains all of the most significant moves in the development of the argument. On the other hand, the small print also contains some of the most interesting material in the *Dogmatics* and in many cases can be read with great profit on its own as well as in conjunction with the main text.

The exegetical and historical content of much of the

small-print material is a reminder of the chief sources for Barth's theology. His appeal is primarily to Scripture and derivatively to the texts and thinkers of the classical Christian tradition. As a theologian of the church, the work of biblical interpretation or exegesis of Scripture is of paramount importance for Barth in the work of theology because he believed that Scripture was the chief instrument through which the gospel of Jesus Christ was published and made known in the world. Exegesis constitutes the attempt to hear what the Spirit of Christ says to the church, and apart from it theology is not able even to begin to discharge its office. Hence, among Barth's last bits of advice concerning theology to his students at Bonn before his departure from Germany was "exegesis, exegesis, exegesis." However, this emphasis on Scripture should not be viewed as being anything like the flat biblicism of many conservative theologies. Such notions of the Bible are inad-

equate for Barth by the very nature of the subject to which the Bible bears witness, the living God revealed in Jesus Christ.

Given the nature of God as the subject of theology, Barth asserts that the discipline must always begin again at the beginning in its attempt to follow and trace the path of the bird in flight. This means we must return to the task of biblical exegesis again and again. However, this work of exegesis does not proceed in isolation from the past witness of the church; due attention must be given to the theological tradition of the church as the witness of past attempts to hear the word of God in Scripture. Indeed, for Barth the notion of dogmatics as *church* dogmatics means that the "theology of past periods, classical and less classical, also plays a part and demands a hearing. It demands a hearing as surely as it occupies a place with us in the context of the Church. The Church does not stand in a vacuum." Therefore, beginning from the beginning "cannot be a matter of beginning off one's own bat. We have to remember the communion of the saints, bearing and being borne by each other, asking and being asked, having to take mutual responsibility for and among the sinners gathered together in Christ. As regards theology, also, we cannot be in the Church without taking as much responsibility for the theology of the past as for the theology of our present."[3] In short, theology must take account of the past attempts at exegesis by those who have gone before us in the faith. At the same time, we must remember that the nature of the subject and the continually changing circumstances in which theological reflection and investigation take place mean that theologians can never be content with simply and uncritically establishing and communicating the results of past theological formulations. Theological reflection and investigation must be renewed constantly.

Drawing on the witness of Scripture and tradition, Barth describes the task of dogmatics in the following way: "Dogmatics is the science in which the Church, in accordance with the state of its knowledge at different times, takes account of the content of its proclamation critically, that is, by the standard of Holy Scripture and under the guidance of its Confessions."[4] The intent of this is to bear witness to the living God revealed in Jesus Christ by saying the same thing in different ways, again and again, always beginning again at the beginning and at every point, from various angles and perspectives, trying to focus on the one who is the totality of the Christian confession. This approach means that Barth offers no system in the *Dogmatics*, but instead seeks to bear witness over and over again to the focal point and foundation of the Christian faith, whose living presence determines that in the work and practice of dogmatics "there are no comprehensive views, no final conclusions and results. There is only the investigation and teaching which take place in the act of dogmatic work and which, strictly speaking, must continually begin again at the beginning in every point. The best and most significant thing that is done in this matter is that again and again we are directed to look back to the center and foundation of it all."[5]

Reading the *Church Dogmatics*

The *Church Dogmatics* is a massive, sprawling work that was written and published over the course of more than thirty years, with the first part-volume appearing in 1932 and the last fragment in the middle of the 1960s, after Barth had retired from teaching. The sheer size of the work, coupled with its dialectical style and rhetorical complexity that resists linear and systematic presentation, make

the interpretation of the *Dogmatics* a challenging under-taking that is resistant to neat summarization. Commenta-tors have often noted the resemblance of its structure to a musical composition; the introduction of a theme is fol-lowed by its development and extension through a lengthy series of explications and recapitulations on various themes that are explored from a variety of angles and contexts. One of the implications of Barth's approach to theology is that no single stage of the argument is definitive and that only the whole conveys the substance of what he is attempting to communicate. The result is that "Barth's views on any given topic cannot be comprehended in a sin-gle statement (even if the statement is one of his own), but only in the interplay of a range of articulations of a theme."[6] Put another way, it is very easy to misread Barth, particularly without careful attention to the shape and style of his work as a whole.

In attempting to help orient readers to the particular chal-lenges of reading the *Church Dogmatics*, George Hunsinger, a well-known interpreter of Barth, has suggested a helpful approach to reading Barth in his book *How to Read Karl Barth*.[7] This work diverges from previous attempts to set forth and analyze Barth with its focus on "pattern recognition" rather than the explication of his theology by means of a "single overriding conception" that functions as the interpretive key to his thought. Hunsinger's aim is to help readers of Barth develop a "set of skills" that will enable them to more effectively discern the argument of the *Church Dogmatics*. He observes that Barth's theology is shaped by the recurrence of several "dialectical and often counterintuitive" patterns or motifs that interlace the argument of the *Dogmatics*. While these patterns are often experienced as elusive and strange to readers of Barth, Hunsinger maintains that they are "fully capable of clear and distinct formulation" and can serve as "felicitous categories of discernment" in the reading of the *Dogmatics*. Since these motifs recur in various contexts and combinations in Barth, the reader who has come to recognize and master them will be better able to grasp the nuances of Barth's argument throughout the *Church Dogmatics* and will also be in a position to appreciate more fully the distinctiveness of his theology.[8] The six motifs identified are actualism, particularism, objectivism, personalism, realism, and rationalism. Let us briefly summarize Hunsinger's work concerning each of these motifs.

Actualism describes Barth's constant use of the language of occurrence, happening, event, history, decision, and act. It means that he thinks primarily in terms of act and relationship, rather than being and substance. For Barth, God's being must always be understood as a being-in-act, meaning that God cannot be described apart from his actions and ongoing active relations. In the same way, the relationship of human beings to God must be conceived only in active, historical terms. Relations with God are not something that can be possessed once and for all, but are rather an event that must be continually established by the ongoing work of grace. Barth's actualism serves to undercut all attempts to understand God and human beings in static categories. Hence, conceptions of Scripture, church, faith, and all other creaturely realities in relationship to God must always be viewed as events that have their being as well as their very possibility only in the free action of God.

Particularism refers to Barth's consistent movement from the particular to the general, rather than from the general to the particular. This approach is demanded because God's revelation in Jesus Christ is utterly unique in kind. As such, no generalities derived from other sources and contexts may properly be applied to theology apart from careful and critical redefinition in light of this particular and unique event. The divine subject matter of theology calls for a radical alteration of conventional discourse and demands that all concepts used in theology must be

developed and defined only on the basis of the particular reality of Jesus Christ. This points to Barth's intention to take his theological bearings strictly from the particularities of the biblical witness and commits him to a high tolerance for mystery.

Objectivism has two important aspects in Barth's thought. First, the knowledge of God confessed by faith is objective in that its basis lies in God and not in human subjectivity. In contrast to the subjective, anthropological approach of much modern Protestant theology, Barth maintains that the identity of God is disclosed in the objective act of God's self-revelation in Christ. In addition, objectivism also means that the action of God in Christ is real, valid, and effective regardless of its positive or negative acknowledgment and reception by human beings.

Personalism points to the reality that God's objective self-manifestation in revelation and salvation comes to human beings in personal form and that human beings respond to God as persons. It is this personalism that enables Barth to maintain his objectivism without developing a disengaged, academic form of theology in which the relationship of human beings to God can appear to be mechanical and impersonal. The objectivist motif establishes the context for the personal encounter between God and human beings and provides the external basis of personalism by asserting that the possibility of relation to God is rooted not in the structure of human nature, but only in the free grace of God mediated by Jesus Christ. Personalism provides the internal basis of objectivism as the goal that objectivism establishes and entails. Through the objective, mediatorial work of Jesus Christ, human beings encounter God personally.

Realism is used to characterize Barth's conception of human language as the vehicle of analogical reference to

God. In itself, human language is radically unlike and insufficient for the task of speaking of God, but by grace God enables it to transcend itself and attain sufficient likeness to make speech about God possible. Thus, for Barth, theological language refers to God by way of analogy. Hence, Barth maintains both the incapacity of human language to refer to God, thus respecting the inherent mystery and otherness of theology's divine subject matter, on the one hand, as well as the possible occurrence of genuine and proper reference to God, on the other, by the miracle of divine self-revelation that allows humans to speak in an authentically informative way about God. This realism can also be described as Barth's doctrine of the "analogy of faith."

Rationalism is the motif that pertains to the construction and assessment of doctrine. It refers to the fact that theology and theological language are understood as having an important rational or cognitive component which is subject to conceptual elaboration. This conceptual elaboration, coupled with biblical exegesis, is at the very center of the theological task. Thus, doctrines may be formulated beyond the basic content of the biblical witness as a means of comprehending the conceptual implications and unity of Scripture. However, because of the unique nature of its subject, the rationalism peculiar to Barth's theology is internal rather than external to faith and might be described as something like reason within the limits of revelation alone. Hunsinger summarizes Barth's theological rationalism with two assertions: "no knowledge without faith" excludes any notion of reliance on reason alone in the task of theology, while "no faith without knowledge" maintains that Christian faith is intrinsically rational.

The significance of Hunsinger's approach is that it preserves the truly dialectical character of Barth's work and

avoids the flattening tendency of systematization characteristic in many interpretations that tend to place emphasis on
a particular aspect of his thought while distorting its general shape. It is the dialectical character of Barth's thought
that makes him seem, at various turns, frustratingly complex, slippery, and even incoherent. Indeed, Hunsinger
maintains that nothing is more likely to lead readers of
Barth astray than a "nondialectical imagination."[9] The
great strength of his book lies in his ability to explicate the

dialectical patterns of Barth's theology in ways that show those patterns to be both comprehensible and coherent, at least within the confines of Barth's particular presentation.

As helpful as the identification of these patterns can be in the task of interpreting and comprehending Barth, readers should be warned that they do not in themselves constitute Barth's theology. Rather, they are the means by which that theology may be better grasped. They do involve material theological decisions, to be sure, but they cannot be used to predict or determine the course and outcome of Barth's argument at any particular point. "It was the subject matter, not the patterns, which Barth was trying to elucidate, and therefore the subject matter by which he wanted his work to be assessed. The patterns were of interest to him only insofar as they were pertinent to illuminating the subject matter. Any pattern might be modified, contradicted, or suppressed in the interest of the subject matter itself."[10] Having said this, let us now turn our attention to a brief overview of the content of each of the volumes of the *Church Dogmatics*.

The Doctrine of the Word of God (*CD* I/1–2)

The first volume of the *Church Dogmatics* contains Barth's prolegomena, or his conception of what must be said first in the articulation of theology. It is an account of what theology is, what it is trying to accomplish, and how it is able to make the claims that it will make. The genre of prolegomena in theological literature emerged in modern Protestantism as a way to establish ground rules for theology. This sort of self-consciousness was a relatively new development in theology in the aftermath of the Enlightenment, which raised questions about the status of theology and whether or not its discourse was in fact even

possible. Hence, instead of launching directly into the subject matter of theology as theologians had done throughout the history of Christian thought, modern theologians engaged in lengthy discussions of method that sought to validate their investigations. The problem with this approach is that theology then has a tendency to get bogged down in preambles. As one observer has quipped, preoccupation with method is like clearing your throat before delivering an address; it can go on only so long before you lose your audience.

Barth addresses this by launching directly into the material content of dogmatics with the assertion that there is no basis for proclamation or theological reflection other than that which is provided by the Word of God itself. The attempts to establish the human conditions that make talk about God possible are seen to be illusory because no such human conditions are possible. Talk about God is possible only because of revelation, and revelation is possible only because God wills it to occur. In the grace and mercy of

God, human speech and language is made to bear witness to the Word of God. As we saw earlier, this is made possible only through the grace of God. Yet that which is humanly impossible is made possible by the will of God, who reveals himself in revelation. God speaks, and, by a miracle enacted by God through the work of the Holy Spirit, this speech is actually heard and received by human beings who are made alive and enabled by the grace and mercy of God to live lives of faith and obedience to God as an act of God's covenant faithfulness.

Barth is able to start at this point because he places theology firmly within the church and thus moves away from understandings of the discipline that seek to transcend the life and faith of the church. "As a theological discipline dogmatics is the scientific self-examination of the Christian Church with respect to the content of its distinctive talk about God."[11] This self-examination and critical evaluation is carried out by the norm of revelation in accordance with the faith and confession of the church. Therefore, dogmatics "does not have to begin by finding or inventing the standard by which it measures. It sees and recognizes that this is given with the Church. It is given in its own peculiar way, as Jesus Christ is given, as God in revelation gives Himself to faith. But it is given. It is complete in itself. It stands by its claim without discussion. It has the certainty which a true standard or criterion must have to be the means of serious measurement."[12] Thus, set within the context of the church, dogmatics is viewed by Barth as an act of faith that moves forward only in constant prayer, apart from which "there can be no dogmatic work."[13] This is because the act of self-examination can be done only through an appeal to the divine act of communication or revelation that produces both the church and its distinctive speech. Thus, Barth begins the *Dogmatics* with a theological examination of the doctrine of the Word of God. He does this in four chapters. In the first chapter, "The Word of God as the Criterion of Dogmatics" (par. 3–7), Barth provides a presentation of his conception of the threefold form of the Word of God. Chapter 2, "The Revelation of God," constitutes an extensive exploration and discussion of Trinitarian theology and is broken down into three component parts: the triune God (par. 8–12), the incarnation of the Word (par. 13–15), and the outpouring of the Holy Spirit (par. 16–18). The presentation concludes with chapters on Scripture (par. 19–21) and the proclamation of the church (par. 22–24).

Perhaps the most significant thing to remember about Barth's theology and his emphasis on the Word of God is that since it is God's Word and not ours, it is never available to us in a direct, straightforward way. It is therefore not to be seen, from Barth's perspective, as a deposit of divine truth from which the church and human beings can draw stable conclusions about God and the world, or a set of propositional statements that can be consulted for information about the divine. Instead, the Word of God is always an *act* that God performs or an *event* in which God has spoken, speaks, and will speak. As human beings we encounter and engage this divine act or event through the human means of Scripture and its proclamation in the church. Hence, the event of the Word of God has three forms: the act of revelation itself, the attestation and witness to revelation in the words of the prophets and the apostles, and the preaching and proclamation of that testimony and witness in the life of the Christian community. In seeking to understand and describe this event, we see a gradual development and progress through three concentric circles that represent three movements in the communication and reception of the Word of God. The innermost circle of the three is the Word of God in its pure form as divine speech-act authored and spoken by God; however, this divine speech or revelation is represented to us and is only expressible and approachable through the human and creaturely speech-acts contained in Scripture and the proclamation of the church. These human speech-acts are appointed by God to become themselves God's Word by derivation, in that they are appointed by God to be the bearers and witnesses of God's self-revelation. Hence, the Word of God is described by Barth as the Word revealed, the Word written, and the Word preached or proclaimed.

In Barth's discussion of the Word of God, it is important to note that he considers not only the divine communication of the Word but also its human reception. Barth makes two important affirmations concerning the human reception of revelation. First, he emphasizes that we cannot think about the event of revelation without remembering at once those who hear it and receive it. In other words, there is a necessary human dimension that is part of our

talk about the Word of God. On the other hand, he reminds us that this human dimension "is not free standing, nor something contributed by the human hearer independent of the event of the Word. Rather, revelation itself creates its own hearers, so (and only so) placing the hearer firmly in the picture. It is because of the directedness of the Word, the fact that God is and acts and speaks *thus*, that talk of God must of necessity include talk of humanity."[14]

Having asserted that the confession "God speaks" is the only proper starting point for theology, Barth turns his attention to an investigation of the God who speaks. Who has spoken? According to Barth, the question of who speaks is answered in Scripture only as it addresses two other crucial questions: what does God speak, and what actually happens when God speaks? In addressing these three questions together—and for Barth they cannot be separated—the church bears witness to its confession of God. "*God* reveals Himself. He reveals Himself *through Himself*. He reveals *Himself*. If we really want to understand revelation in terms of its subject, God, the Revealer, is identical with His act in revelation and also identical with its effect. It is from this fact, which in the first instance we are merely indicating, that we learn we must begin the doctrine of revelation with the doctrine of the triune God."[15] Barth ties together the confession of the church that God is triune with the very structure of revelation and asserts that the reason for the confession of the church concerning the Trinitarian nature of God is that this is the way in which God is revealed to us. In other words, revelation has an inherently Trinitarian structure because God is triune. In speaking his Word, the hidden, ineffable God reveals himself to us; in sending his Son, God becomes the Revelation itself; and in sending his Spirit, God makes himself effectively known to human beings. "God is the Subject of revelation, and always in such a way that he remains Subject. God is the Revelation itself, the 'other' in whom he both knows himself and makes himself known to creatures. And God is the historical effectiveness of his revelation, the lively response evoked by this event. In short, God is Father, Son, and Holy Spirit, and only in the occurrence of all three taken together does revelation happen."[16] As Barth puts it at the opening of his discussion of the revelation of God, "God's Word is God Himself in His revelation. For God reveals Himself as the Lord and according to Scripture this signifies for the concept of revelation that God Himself in unimpaired unity yet also in unimpaired distinction is Revealer, Revelation, and Revealedness."[17]

Barth's doctrine of revelation is captured in the language of "indirect identity" and the dialectic of veiling and unveiling. This means that in his self-revelation God makes himself to be indirectly identical with the creaturely medium of revelation, such as the human nature of Jesus or the language of Scripture. Such revelation is *indirect* because God's use of the creaturely medium entails no "divinization" of the medium, and its inherent limitations remain; yet at the same time God is indirectly *identical* with the creaturely medium in that God chooses to truly *reveal* himself through such mediums. This is the dialectic of veiling and unveiling which maintains that God unveils (reveals) himself in and through creaturely veils, and that these veils, although they be used of God for the purposes of unveiling himself, remain veils. Further, the self-revelation of God means that the whole of God, complete and entire, and not simply a part, is made known in revelation, but nevertheless remains hidden within the veil of the creaturely medium through which he chooses to unveil himself. Hence, nothing of God is known directly by natural human perception.

With respect to the revelation of God in Jesus Christ, this means that the process by which God takes on human nature and becomes the subject of a human life in human history entails no impartation or communication of divine attributes and perfections to that human nature. Hence, revelation does not become a predicate of the human nature of Jesus and therefore revelation may not be read directly from Jesus. Likewise, the use God makes of the words of the prophets and apostles entails no impartation or communication of divine attributes and perfections to those words. They remain subject to their inherent limitations as a creaturely medium. The consequence of this notion of indirect revelation is that it remains hidden to outward, normal, or "natural" human perception and requires that human beings be given "the eyes and ears of faith" in order to perceive the unveiling of God that remains hidden in the creaturely veil. In this conception, revelation has both an objective moment, when God reveals himself through the veil of a creaturely medium, and a subjective moment, when God gives human beings the faith to understand what is hidden in the veil. The objective moment occurs in Jesus Christ, while the subjective moment occurs through the work of the Holy Spirit.

In this framework of indirect identity, we are able to affirm God's use of human language in the act of revelation without denying our theological and existential awareness of its inherent limitations and contingencies as a contextually situated creaturely medium. It should be added that Barth secures the divine primacy in God's epistemic (related to knowledge or knowing) relations with human beings by maintaining the "actualistic" character of revelation. In other words, revelation in this conception is not simply a past event that requires nothing further from God. This would imply that God had ceased to act and become directly identical with the medium of revelation. If this were the case, the epistemic relationship between God and human beings would be static rather than dynamic, with the result that human beings would be able to move from a position of epistemic dependency to one of epistemic mastery. Instead, God always remains indirectly identical with the creaturely mediums of revelation, thus requiring continual divine action in the knowing process and securing the ongoing dependency of human beings with respect to the knowledge of God. In other words, as human beings we are *always and at every point* dependent on God for our knowledge of God.

The Doctrine of God (*CD* II/1–2)

In this volume Barth builds on his assertion that theology has no other basis than God's self-revelation as Father, Son, and Holy Spirit with a detailed discussion of the doctrine of God. Barth's presentation provides an account of God's being that adheres to the rule that God is as God acts. The volume is divided into two major movements. The first, in *CD* II/1, sets forth an account of God as agent or actor whose being is identical with the activity of loving in freedom. God is as God does, and what God does is love. This movement culminates in a discussion of the attributes or perfections of God based on the actions of God. The second movement, in *CD* II/2, considers the particular action, performed by God and deeply indicative of the

being and character of God, the act of gracious election. The two parts of Barth's presentation form an exposition of God's character in relation to humanity as the One who loves in freedom. This discussion falls into four sections: the knowledge of God (par. 25–27); the reality of God (par. 28–31); the election of God (par. 32–35); and the command of God (par. 36–39).

At the outset of this volume, Barth returns to the idea of the knowledge of God to drive home the point that he has made again and again throughout his writings: God is not at our disposal. To speak of the human knowledge of God requires that God make that which is impossible from the human standpoint possible by an act of grace. Here Barth speaks of the fulfillment of the knowledge of God rather than the possibility of such knowledge. The knowledge of God is brought to fulfillment or completion by the work of the Spirit. In other words, Barth asserts the gracious reality that God is known before investigating how this is possible. The challenge is to maintain the reality of this knowledge for human beings while also ensuring that God always remains the acting subject who is always free in relation to human beings. The knowledge of God is not made available to us in such a way that it enters into our control; it is always an event and never something that humans can claim as a secure possession. Hence, the knowledge of God that is made known to human beings is both objective (it is the genuine knowledge of God that is made known) and dynamic (it cannot be possessed by human beings once for all). We are always dependent on God, from moment to moment, for our knowledge of God.

One of the entailments of this is Barth's vigorous denial of natural theology, the idea that there is some knowledge of God that is generally available outside of revelation. According to Barth such notions must always be rejected as compromising the Creator-creature distinction. To seek some common ground between believers and nonbelievers that can be the basis for an apologetic defense of Christian faith is to suggest that the knowledge of God is generally available to humans as humans, and this cannot be, from Barth's perspective. The problem is not that believers have the knowledge of God while unbelievers do not; far from it. The central conviction for Barth is that no human possesses the knowledge of God, so the impossibility of natural theology is another way of bearing witness to the radical dependence of human beings on the grace of God. The goal in all of this is to shift the tendency in theology to begin with ourselves and then move onto God. Barth seeks to reverse this modern intuition and insist that we must begin with God.

As Barth's discussion shifts from the knowledge of God to the reality of God, he asserts that the most fundamental preoccupation of Christian dogmatics is the explication of the statement "God is." The concern here is not the possibility of the existence of God, but the character of God. In keeping with the denial of natural theology, we must set aside all of our assumptions and preconceptions concerning what we already believe to be true of God and instead seek to learn solely from the God who is. For Barth, to say "God is" means that "God acts" and that the most basic category for understanding the being of God is agency. Therefore, Barth moves immediately to a consideration of the works of God, which are the manifestation of the identity of God. God is known through what God has done, and what God has done emerges from the witness of Scripture. What we see in the pages of Scripture is that God is the One who loves in freedom. Two points need to be made here. First, Barth seeks to expound the biblical assertion that "God is love" and work it thoroughly into the

substance of all his theology through an examination of the specific and active character of God's love. As with our understanding of God, we must not presume that we know the character of love in advance and then impose that on the love of God. The specific way in which God loves is through the ongoing establishment of communion between God and God's creatures. God's love for the world is not that of a passionless Deity, but rather that of one who is passionately involved in the life of the world, and pours out this love lavishly in Jesus Christ.

However, this love is qualified by the fact that God is not simply the One who loves, but more fully, the One who loves in freedom. Here God's transcendent power and majesty are on display in such a way that God is understood as wholly other than finite human creatures. That God loves in freedom underscores that God loves us in the way that God wills, that God is completely sovereign. However, this sovereignty is not to be viewed simply as the assertion that God can do whatever God desires, but rather that what God does in freedom is love. For Barth, the love of God and the freedom of God cannot be abstracted from each other without doing violence to each of the concepts, the identity of God and the character of God's love. God's love is "utterly free, grounded in itself, needing no other, and yet also not lacking in another, but in sovereign transcendence giving, communicating itself to the other. In this freedom it is the divine loving. But we must also say, conversely, that only in this divine loving is the freedom described by us divine freedom: If we abstract the love of God and therefore the purpose of God, however circumspect we may be, we describe only a world-principle."[18] The life of God as the One who loves in freedom is infinitely textured and complex in its numerous and varied perfections, which Barth discusses in detail in paragraphs 29–31.

The identity of God as the One who loves in freedom finds its culmination in the gracious action of election. As Barth turns his attention to this classical Reformed doctrine he says:

> The doctrine of election is the sum of the Gospel because of all words that can be said or heard it is the best: that God elects man; that God is for man too the One who loves in freedom. It is grounded in the knowledge of Jesus Christ because He is both the electing God and the elected man in One. It is part of the doctrine of God because originally God's election of man is a predestination not merely of man but of Himself. Its function is to bear basic testimony to eternal, free and unchanging grace as the beginning of all the ways and works of God.[19]

Here the culmination of Barth's argument concerning God is brought to bear fruitfully on the doctrine of election, which is not in his hands an investigation into the machinations of the divine mind who sorts humanity into the categories of the saved and the damned, but instead is the very best word of all, for in the act of election we discover that God is God *for* us.

Election is focused on the reality of Jesus Christ, who is understood by Barth to be both "electing and elected." Barth appeals to the two natures of Jesus Christ as divine and human in order to reshape the notion of double predestination to God's self-election and God's election of humanity, which are both actual in Jesus Christ. In Christ we are able to conceptualize election as divine self-election. Here any sense of arbitrary divine omnipotence is excluded from an understanding of the will of God, since what is important is specificity of God's will, and God elects to be God known in and as Jesus Christ. "In the beginning with God was this One, Jesus Christ. And that is predestination. All that this concept contains and comprehends is to be found originally in Him and must be understood in relation to Him."[20] In Jesus Christ we see that God's self-election is his determination to be gracious and that this grace is not merely one mode or modulation of an absolute will which could be directed in other ways or for other ends. In Jesus Christ we are also able to discern election as the election of humanity, in that the agent of election is Jesus Christ himself and that the means of this election is the sharing of our humanity by Christ in the incarnation. Barth also asserts that this implies an affirmation that election is to the form of human life established by Jesus. Election is election to participate in the covenant life made possible in Jesus Christ.

The result of Barth's restatement of election is an understanding of the electing God and elect humanity in which election "is not fate but form. Election and ethics are thus inseparable, since humanity is elect not simply to a state but a way of life. Election is purposive determination, determination to blessedness, gratitude and service as witness."[21] For this reason Barth concludes his consideration of the doctrine of God with a final chapter on ethics and the moral implications of the doctrine. For Barth, the Christian concept of the covenant of God with humanity includes the doctrine of election as its first element and the doctrine of God's command as its second. And it is only in this conception of the covenant that the doctrine of God can find completion. "For God is not known and is not knowable except in Jesus Christ. He does not exist in His divine being and perfections without Jesus Christ, in whom he is both very God and very man. He does not exist, therefore, without the covenant with man which was made and executed in His name. God is not known completely—and therefore not at all—if He is not known as the Maker and Lord of this covenant between himself and man." In light of this reality, the Christian understanding of God cannot concern only God since its focus is on this particular God; it must also include humanity, to the extent that in Jesus Christ humanity "is made a partner in the covenant decreed and founded by God."[22]

The Doctrine of Creation (*CD* III/1–4)

In the third volume of the *Dogmatics*, Barth develops his doctrine of creation with a discussion of God as the Creator and lengthy expositions of the creation narratives in the first two chapters of Genesis in the first part-volume (*CD* III/1). In the second (*CD* III/2), he turns his attention to an understanding of the human person or theological anthropology and what it means for humans to be created in the image of God. The third part-volume (*CD*

III/3) takes up the question of providence, while the final part-volume (*CD* III/4) consists of Barth's development of the ethics of creation.

From Barth's perspective, the Christian doctrine of creation is concerned with faith in God the Creator and simply with the question of origins. This doctrine, like all others for Barth, concerns God and investigates the identity of God as the Creator. Like all Christian reflection, the consideration and reflection on creation takes place in the realm of the church and begins with the confession of the creed that God is the Creator. Hence, the doctrine of creation "no less than the whole remaining content of Christian confession is an article of faith, i.e., the rendering of a knowledge which no man has procured for himself or ever will; which is neither native to him nor accessible to him by way of observation and logical thinking; for which he has no organ and no ability; which he can in fact achieve only in faith; but which is actually consummated in faith, i.e., in the reception of and response to the divine witness."[23] In making this move Barth seeks to shift the center of gravity in our conception of creation away from the consciousness of existence that we have as human beings and toward the free self-existence of God. In other words, for Barth, all of theological reflection must properly begin with God. Further, our knowledge of God as creator of all that is derives from our knowledge of Jesus Christ. "I believe in Jesus Christ, God's Son our Lord, in order to perceive and to understand that God the Almighty, the Father, is the Creator of heaven and earth. If I did not believe the former, I could not perceive and understand the latter."[24]

This strongly christological orientation toward creation has the function of providing "a distinctly teleological character to the doctrine of creation; the created order can be understood only in the light of God's purposes for creation enacted in Jesus Christ and made real in the power of the Holy Spirit. The creation *is* (and therefore is known as) that reality which God destines for fellowship with Jesus Christ. And, because of this, 'creation' and 'covenant' are correlative terms."[25] The exploration of the close connection of creation and covenant forms the longest section of *CD* III/1 and contains two extended exegetical examinations of the creation accounts in Genesis 1–2. This discussion is developed around two focal concerns: First, that creation forms the external basis of God's covenant with humanity, in that God's work of creation always has in view "the institution, preservation, and execution of the covenant of grace, for partnership in which he has predestined and called man."[26] Second, the covenant is the internal basis of creation, meaning that God's covenant with humanity constitutes the fulfillment of the very intentions of God in the work of creation. In this presentation, creation is viewed as the first in a series of works of the triune God and so must be viewed and understood in the context of the Trinity. "Indeed, it is only a doctrine of the Trinity which can prevent us from thinking either that creation is a quasi-independent act of God unrelated to the work of salvation, or that salvation-history can be abstracted from the work of God in which the world and humanity are willed and brought into being."[27] In this conception, Trinity, creation, and covenant must therefore be seen together as indissolubly united in the being and action of God as well as in the understanding of the church in its confession of God as the maker of heaven and earth.

In turning his attention to theological anthropology, or the nature of the human person, Barth follows a pattern similar to his conception of creation in the attempt to understand humanity in the light of Jesus Christ. The pivotal question concerns the biblical witness that human beings are created in the *imago Dei*, the image of God. What does this mean? Throughout the history of Christian reflection and teaching concerning this assertion, many notions have been suggested to describe the image, such as the presence of an immortal soul, the possession of reason, or the capacity for dominion. Rather than pursuing these options, Barth turns his attention to Jesus, who is depicted in the New Testament as the image of the invisible God through whom and for whom all things have been created (Col. 1:15–16). For Barth, this means that the image of God is not something that human beings possess as a constituent part of their nature. Instead, the image of God is Jesus Christ, the one in whom the destiny of all creation will be fulfilled. The image of God is not an attribute of humanity so much as it is the relationship that humans bear to the true human, Jesus Christ. This points to the reason for which God engaged in the act of creation, namely, to pour out love and grace on humanity in the person of Jesus Christ. Creation is therefore the gift of God in Christ, but must always be ordered toward its consummation in Christ. Hence, creation is dependent on the specific and particular reality of the person of God's Son, Jesus Christ, who is both its beginning and its end. As such, human beings find their true humanity only in relationship to God through Christ, who is the one through whom and for whom they have been made.

In his doctrine of creation, Barth has provided a description of the triune God as the agent of creation who brings into being another reality, that which is not God, and establishes a covenant relationship for love, grace, and blessing. Barth's understanding of the human creature provides an account of creatureliness as that reality which is destined, equipped, and established for fellowship with God through Jesus Christ. Barth concludes this section by drawing these two themes together in an account of providence that may be viewed as the ongoing history of creation. Christian faith confesses God as the Creator who brings all things into being; the Christian confession of providence maintains that the God of creation does not abandon the world, but instead lovingly and graciously guides it toward its intended goal in Christ. "The doctrine of providence deals with the history of created beings as such, in the sense that in every respect and in its whole span this proceeds under the fatherly care of God the Creator, whose will is done and is to be seen in his election of grace, and therefore in the history of the covenant between himself and man, and therefore in Jesus Christ."[28]

Barth does not view providence primarily in terms of the general oversight and governance of creation, but rather as a function of God's eternal determination to be God for us in Jesus Christ. Barth further encapsulates his understanding of providence with the assertion that in the act of creation "God the Creator as such has associated Himself with His creature as such as the Lord of its history, and is faithful to it as such."[29] Therefore, the content of providence is the continuing, historical fellowship that God initiates and sustains in Jesus Christ with the created order and his creatures over which he is Lord. Barth does not offer a doctrine of providence in which God is pictured as the one who causes all things to occur. In fact, "Barth takes great pains to guard against all merely mechanical or deterministic understandings of God's rule. God neither coerces creatures, nor lives their lives for them, nor cuts them loose to find their own way; that would suggest a zero-sum game, in which God and creatures are forced to compete for scant resource of agency or power. That is scarcely the picture of God's care for the world seen in the Bible."[30]

The character of Barth's investigation does not lead him to a resolution of the problem of divine providence and human freedom. What he does provide, following the pattern he sees in Scripture, is a series of particular descriptions of divine and human agency that respect the biblical witness of each, while at the same time also avoiding a theoretical closure that would raise questions about the integrity of either. From Barth's perspective, while it is true that we are unable to provide resolutions or explanations as to the ways in which divine and human agency cohere, it does not follow that we are being inconsistent or incoherent in our affirmation of both. We must simply be as faithful as possible to the witness of Scripture and acknowledge the mystery that pertains to the particularity of the revelation of God in Jesus Christ.

The Doctrine of Reconciliation (*CD* IV/1–4)

Reconciliation is the word Barth uses to describe the complex event that occurred in Jesus and to integrate the person of Christ with the work of Christ. However, Barth's doctrine of reconciliation moves the discussion well beyond the traditional parameters of reflection on the person and work of Jesus, although these remain central to its concerns. In addition to an investigation of incarnation, the cross, and resurrection, Barth's presentation also includes discussions of the Spirit, the church, sin, salvation, ethics, and the Christian life. In its holistic and extensive engagement with a wide variety of themes often not addressed in more traditional theological discussions of

Christ, Barth's work can be read as an attempt to see all things connected in Christ through an extended commentary on the biblical proclamation that "in Christ God was reconciling the world to himself" (2 Cor. 5:19). Barth began his work on this volume, which would be his last, at the age of 65, well aware of the significance of this particular topic in the context of his overall project and vision. In the foreword to the first part-volume he writes: "I have been very conscious of the very special responsibility laid on the theologian at this centre of all Christian knowledge. To fail here is to fail everywhere. To be on the right track here makes it impossible to be completely mistaken in the whole. Week by week and even day by day I have had, and will have (in the continuation), to exercise constant vigilance to find the right track and not lose it."[31]

The structure of this volume is quite complex, such that no section of the presentation is definitive, with each building on and expanding the others, so that it is important to read the volume as a whole rather than as a series of separate and discrete developments. The three tracts of argument in IV/1, IV/2, and IV/3 each follow a similar structure with a different focal point, and together they form a carefully developed and orchestrated series of articulations, repetitions, echoes, and variations. Each of these part-volumes begins with a detailed treatment of the person and work of Christ viewed from a different angle of vision. Barth is quite insistent that Christ's person and work are interdependent relations which cannot be expounded in isolation from each other. They are not to be separated, because it is the nature of Christ to be in action. On the one hand, we cannot know the person of Christ apart from the performance of his work. On the other hand, we would not properly know the work of Christ if we did not see his person as the irreplaceable subject of that work. Hence, while we must not *separate* Christ's person and work, it is important to *distinguish* between them in order to make it clear that in Jesus we have an authentic divine-human advocate who acts on our behalf through his pure and gracious initiative.

In his exposition, Barth draws together three stands of classical Christian teaching and confession concerning Jesus: first, the idea formulated by the ecumenical Council of Chalcedon in response to questions about the being of Jesus, that he is both fully God and fully human, true God and true humanity in one person; second, the two states of humiliation and exaltation that characterize Jesus in the work of reconciliation; and third, the offices of priest, king, and prophet that are fulfilled in Jesus. Part-volume IV/1 considers the person and work of Christ from the perspective of the Lord as Servant and describes the obedience of Jesus, the Son of God, with respect to his willingness to set aside the prerogatives of his divinity and take judgment upon himself. Here Barth ties together the obedience of Christ with his deity and his execution of the priestly office,

with the effect of focusing on the lowliness of the incarnate Son of God in relation to the being of God and driving that humility into the divine life. In IV/2 Barth follows a similar pattern, explicating the person and work of Christ again, only this time from the perspective of Jesus Christ, the Servant as Lord. Here the paradox of divinity in humility from IV/1 is reversed and the humanity of Christ is related to triumph and exaltation and the fulfillment of the office of king. The way in which Barth's presentation is organized is counterintuitive, subverting the common assumption that the divine nature, the state of exaltation, and the kingly office should be taken up and considered together on the one hand, while the human nature, the state of humiliation, and the priestly office should be developed on the other.

In IV/3 Barth rounds off his presentation with an explicit investigation into the unity of the two natures of divinity and humanity in Christ, and the unity of the two states of humility and exaltation. He does this through a consideration of Jesus Christ as the true witness who is the light of the world in his prophetic office. In summary, then, Barth's presentation of Jesus Christ as the reconciler looks like this: Jesus Christ is revealed as being truly and fully God in his willingness to endure humiliation for our sake in the fulfillment of his priestly action toward us as the one who stands in our place; Jesus Christ is revealed as truly and fully human in his exaltation to fellowship with God in the fulfillment of his kingly office; and Jesus Christ is revealed as one person, divine and human, in that, through the Holy Spirit, he gives himself to us and for us as the pledge and witness of who he is and what he does in the fulfillment of his prophetic office.

In conjunction with this integrated and holistic account of the person and work of Jesus Christ, or preferably, the being-in-act of Jesus Christ as the divine-human agent of reconciliation, Barth examines a particular aspect of the effect of Christ's reconciling work addressing, overcoming, and healing the alienation of humanity from God. As the obedient Son of God, Jesus Christ exposes the sin of pride, which leads to the downfall of humanity, in his willingness to endure humiliation and judgment. As the victorious Son of Man, he lays bare the sin of sloth that refuses to take notice of and be transfixed by his triumph and exaltation and thus leads to a continuation in misery and despair. As the true witness, Jesus exposes the sin of falsehood which turns from the light of truth to the darkness of a lie that leads to condemnation. In each of these cases, sin is understood as rebellion against the movement of the grace of God that embraces and heals human life.

However, this rebellion can only be understood as such in the light of the grace which it so obstinately opposes. For Barth, sin is not so much simply wrong conduct over against the law as it is opposition to the very grace and love of the God who seeks to reconcile the world to himself in Christ. Sin is, then, "not only that which is forbidden, but that which has no grounding at all, and it is in its presumptuous reality so incredibly empty that the divine reconciliation alone is a match for it. It can only be truly known where God in his kindness sets himself in opposition to it. It must therefore be discussed after Christology, not before."[32] In describing the ways in which the work of God in Christ heals the damage done by sin and effects the renewal of human life, Barth expounds it in the classical

language of justification (par. 61) and sanctification (par. 66), and in a lengthy discussion of the vocation of humanity to be witnesses of God's reconciliation in Christ. The appropriation of this divine renewal or salvation is viewed by Barth as the work of the Spirit in the gathering of the community (par. 62), the building up of the community (par. 67), and the sending of the community (par. 72). The focus on community underscores that divine renewal or salvation is made known first to the Christian community, meaning that individuals can be "Christians" only in the community of Christ's followers. However, the church does not mediate salvation to individuals (remember Barth's critique of the Catholic tradition with respect to the nature of grace). Hence, there is only a provisional difference between Christians and all others in that Christians know of the salvation and renewal of Christ's reconciling work and they are charged with bearing witness to its reality in the world. The structure of Barth's presentation concludes with the work of the Spirit in the appropriation of salvation through the generation of faith (par. 63), love (par. 68), and hope (par. 73).

Barth had given thought to calling this volume the doctrine of the covenant in order to underscore its inner theme, summarized in the biblical witness to "Immanuel, God with us," which is captured in the classical designation of Jesus Christ as "true God and true human" and serves as a description of the divine covenant made in Jesus Christ. This covenant is not most properly viewed as a new covenant, but rather as the fulfillment of the covenant made by God with Israel, which is now completed and extended to all people in Christ. Finally, it must be remembered that for Barth this covenantal fulfillment in Christ is not to be understood as a reaction to human sin and rebellion, but rather as the working out of the original goodwill that God intended for his creatures from the beginning as the One who loves in freedom and is "for us" from eternity. In the end, Barth's doctrine of reconciliation stands as one of the great theological treatises in the history of Christian thought, a powerful and compelling intellectual and literary witness to the heart of the gospel, that in Christ God was indeed reconciling all things to himself.

Ethics

Barth always asserted that one of the important features of the Reformed theological tradition was its emphasis on the importance of morals and right living. Because of this commitment to moral reflection, the *Church Dogmatics* contains a twofold emphasis on dogmatics and ethics corresponding to the covenantal relationship between God and humanity. However, Barth's presentation of ethics is quite different from what we typically think of when we consider the subject of ethics. From Barth's perspective, the discipline of modern ethics is governed by presuppositions and assumptions that are at odds with Christian convictions. This is seen in the fundamental inquiry of modern ethics in its various forms, "What should *I* do?" To begin with this question is to set human beings at the center of the created order and suggests the autonomy of human beings in ethical reflection. Traditional conceptions of ethics are about the human project and the attempt to define and determine the good from the perspective of human beings. Barth asserts that from the perspective of Christian faith, this entire approach to moral reflection rests on the false assumption that the question of the good can be considered and addressed apart from the reality of the living God. If ethics is to be properly Christian, it must be appropriately theological, in that it begins with God and

the actions of God and only then turns to consider the implications of this for human beings and their moral choices.

For Barth the properly theological character of ethics means that they should be treated in the context of dogmatics. In particular, Barth maintains that ethical reflection must take place in the context of the ways in which the triune God engages with humanity as the Creator, the Reconciler, and the Redeemer. This Trinitarian pattern shapes the structure of Barth's presentation of ethics in the *Dogmatics*: in the context of the doctrine of God, Barth provides his presentation of general theological ethics in *CD* II/2, chapter 8, "The Command of God"; *CD* III/4 sets forth the ethics of creation; *CD* IV/4 begins the ethics of reconciliation that Barth did not live to complete; the ethics of redemption would have rounded out Barth's presentation had he been able to write the projected fifth volume.

Barth's location of general ethics in the doctrine of God marks a distinct contrast with the assumption that ethics is primarily about human beings. Barth asserts that ethics begins with God and that the moral law is another form of the gospel situated in the electing grace of God. "As the doctrine of God's command, ethics interprets the Law as the form of the Gospel, i.e., as the sanctification which comes to man through the electing God."[33] In light of this, the first thing we must say about ethics and the moral quest is that human life unfolds in a context that is shaped and determined by the grace of God in Jesus Christ. Before we make any determination with regard to our actions or before we engage in any activity, we function in a context in which we have been freed for covenant fellowship with God and our neighbor. To assert that the law is a form of the gospel means that the law is subordinate to grace, since grace is fundamental to the gospel. Further, in Barth's conception it stands as an assertion against any notions of natural law that may be known apart from the divine revelation of the gospel. Ethics, in other words, must begin with Jesus and not some other supposed foundation in human experience. At the same time, the assertion that the law is a form of the gospel works against any conceptions of grace that deny the moral obligations of the gospel. The grace of God revealed in the gospel includes the sanctification of human beings through obedience to God's commandments.

In addition to connecting Christian ethics to the gospel, Barth also expounds on the idea of the command of God as the norm for Christian ethics. For Barth, Christ is the content of God's commandment, and knowing how to act in a particular situation means attending to what God has to say in Christ. This is not something that can be known or determined in advance by general knowledge or experience. The problem with humanity is that we often think we know what is "good" and thus pursue a particular course

of action, oblivious to the ways in which our very notions of the good are corrupted and serve our own ends. "Breaking the closed circle of human certainty requires that we attend to what God is saying, not 'normalizing' the commandment by assimilating it to what we already know, but allowing our moral imaginations to be stretched. The good is never simply 'the natural,' but must be *learned*, and that through an encounter with the Word that the Word itself makes possible."[34] For Christians the good is not constituted by an idea or a principle, but by God, who wills that we should be morally responsible partners in the covenant of grace and reconciliation. In Barth's conception, Christian ethics has more to do with the surprises that are part of the ongoing drama of human existence than with the certainties of a stable system.

In other words, for Barth the command of God is always an event and never simply a directive that can be formalized into something statutory. It is an episode or an incident in an ongoing series in the history of God's relation to us. This is because Jesus is the content of the divine command. "What God wills of us is the same as he wills and has done for us. God wills Jesus. This is how he directs His demand to us. This is how He claims us for Himself. It is well to consider the matter in this simplest possible formulation. All explanations of what it means in detail can only return continually to this simplest formula." We are in constant need of the light that streams from Jesus and this simplest form of the truth. "The name of Jesus is itself the designation of the divine content of the divine claim, of the substance of God's law."[35] In stating the matter this way, Barth is not simply claiming that the moral teaching of Jesus is at the center of Christian ethics and the Christian life; instead, he is referring to action instead of instruction. The notion that the name of Jesus is the content of the divine command means that the history of Jesus and his actions sum up and complete the covenant God makes with humanity. Giving ethical primacy to the name of Jesus is making the claim that ethical reality, including the moral worlds in which we live, the nature of our own sense of morality, and particularly the God whose command we encounter in the covenant of grace and reconciliation, is defined at every point by the action of Jesus Christ. "Acting in God's stead and in our stead, Jesus establishes moral truth; good human action is action which corresponds to that truth. God's command is not merely that we should submit to a power, but that we should act in conformity with the reality of God's gracious history with us."[36]

The assertions that the law is a form of the gospel and that the name of Jesus constitutes the content of the divine command lead us to see the grace of God in the existence of Jesus Christ and his people through the establishment and fulfillment of the covenant. From this perspective and, according to Barth, only from this perspective are we in a position to provide an appropriately Christian and theological answer to the question of proper ethical and moral standards and conduct. "What are we to do? We are to do what corresponds to this grace. We are to respond to the existence of Jesus Christ and His people. With our action we are to render an account to this grace. By it and by it alone we are challenged. To it and to it alone we are responsible."[37]

CHAPTER SEVEN

Barth's Legacy

Retirement

By the time Barth retired from teaching in March 1962, he was widely regarded as one of the most important theologians in the history of the Protestant tradition, joining the select company of names like Martin Luther, John Calvin, and Friedrich Schleiermacher. His thought had received ongoing attention since the publication of the Romans commentary, and this only intensified with the steady stream of volumes that made up the *Church Dogmatics,* along with his numerous other writings. His production of written material was so prolific that the prominent Roman Catholic theologian Hans Urs von Balthasar referred to him as an "eternal cornucopia."[1] However, as mentioned earlier, Barth was unable to complete the *Dogmatics* and never even started on the final volume in the series.

In his last years, he was often asked about the nonappearance of the remaining parts of the *Dogmatics*. He sometimes responded to these queries by asking whether the material that was already available had been read and studied, and if so, how much and how thoroughly. On other occasions he noted the incomplete nature of the great medieval theologies, such as that of Thomas Aquinas, and of many cathedrals. And sometimes he quipped that since perfection is the epitome of the divine attributes, it is better not to seek it or attempt to imitate it in a human work; hence it was better to leave the *Dogmatics* in its imperfect and unfinished state rather than attempting to finish it. However, he concluded, "Naturally these were and are excuses, and rather presumptuous ones as far as comparisons are concerned. They conceal the simple fact that I have gradually begun to lose the physical energy and mental drive necessary to continue and complete the work which I started . . . it is indeed too late to do this in worthy fashion."[2]

Unfinished or not, Barth never viewed the *Dogmatics* as an attempt at having the last word in theology, which he regarded as an impossibility; rather, he saw the work not as a conclusion but as the opening of a new conversation concerning the proper direction for theology. Thus, in his last lectures, Barth ended his formal teaching career by striking the same notes with which he had started and sustained it, saying of theological work and its direction, "Anyone who sets out to do it can never proceed by building with complete confidence on questions which have already been settled, results which have already been achieved or conclusions which are already assured. He is directed every day, indeed every hour, to begin again *at the beginning*."[3]

Part of the challenge of coming to terms with Barth's theology during his lifetime, in addition to the sheer volume of his own work, was also what he referred to as the "terrifying" number of books that had been written about his thought in both the European and North American contexts. He observed that few theologians had ever been the object of so much research and description during their lifetime and that this occasionally made him feel as though he was someone who had contracted a particularly interesting ailment and was therefore "surrounded on the operating table by numerous older and younger dignitaries in white coats, and having to listen now to this one and now to that saying what he has discovered, according to the degree of his professional understanding, about the make-up and condition of my various organs and their origins in my earlier history."[4] Yet in spite of his attempt to articulate and exemplify his approach to theology in the *Dogmatics* and his other writings, and in spite of the numerous studies of his thought that were becoming available, Barth remained concerned that while many had taken up the reading and study of his work and commented on it in detail, his prescriptions concerning the direction for theology were not, for various reasons, being followed. He concluded that his work, particularly the *Church Dogmatics*, would have to wait for its time.

Karl Barth died in Basel on December 10, 1968. In the aftermath of his death, interest in his theology gradually began to wane, such that by the beginning of the 1990s it could be written with justification that Barth had "achieved the dubious distinction of being habitually honored but not much read."[5]

Barth Revived

Ten years later, at the beginning of the twenty-first century, the situation has changed considerably and there is now ample evidence of a revival of interest in the study of Barth. In recent years a steady stream of books, articles, and dissertations have been produced that provide commentary on Barth's theology; the Karl Barth Society of North America is flourishing; and the newly established Center for Barth Studies at Princeton Theological Seminary is promoting scholarly and ecclesial engagement with his thought. The most important development is that Barth is again being read, and read extensively.

At least two reasons account for this resurgence of interest in Barth's thought. The first is simply the concern of historical scholarship to gain purchase on a more accurate conception of what Barth was in fact attempting to say in his work. Over the past twenty-five years the Swiss edition of Barth's collected writings has made generally available a large quantity of important and previously unpublished material, such as lectures, sermons, and letters. Of particular importance are the lecture cycles from the early years of Barth's career as a theology professor. The availability of these writings has provided the opportunity to carefully examine the development of Barth's thought. This critical scrutiny has led to significant revisions in the standard profile of that development, particularly the notion that Barth abandoned the dialectical thinking characteristic of his early theology. This has, in turn, led to important alterations concerning the precise contours of his mature theology contained in the *Church Dogmatics.*

The second reason for this renewed interest in Barth

may be found in the new opportunities for theology arising out of the shifting cultural climate. As we venture into
the twenty-first century, the discipline of theology is in a
state of transition and ferment brought about by the breakdown of the assumptions of the modern world spawned by
the Enlightenment. This breakdown has led to the emergence of postmodern thought, with its withering critique
of the modern, scientific quest for certain, objective, and
universal knowledge and its attempt to engage in new
forms of discourse in the aftermath of modernity. This
postmodern attempt to construct new paradigms for
knowledge and intellectual pursuit has significantly shaped
the discipline of theology in the past decade as theologians
from various contexts and traditions have sought to "fill
the void" left by the perceived failure of modernity. Sur-
prisingly and somewhat ironically, the thought of Karl
Barth has come to be closely associated with several of
these recent attempts to rethink theology after modernity.
The perceived affinity of Barth's theology with some of the
intellectual tendencies of postmodernism has led some
interpreters to suggest that Barth, who considered himself
both a child and a critic of the nineteenth century, may find
his greatest influence in the century to come.

We will briefly mention two approaches to reading
Barth's work that are prominent in current North American conceptions of Barth: neo-orthodox interpretations,
with their positive emphasis on the "givenness" of revelation and the knowledge of God; and postmodern interpretations, with their emphasis on the absolute "otherness" of
God and the "nongivenness" of revelation. The importance of Barth's theology for these proposals points to the
ongoing significance of his thought in the construction of
contemporary theology and to the variety of ways in which
aspects of his thought have been developed.

Readings of Barth: Neo-orthodox and Postmodern

The dominant approach to reading Barth's work in the English-speaking world is that of neo-orthodoxy. The designation suggests the ways in which Barth's theology constitutes a revisioning of the older Protestant orthodoxy while taking on board some of the insights of the modern world. In this interpretation of Barth, some of the major themes of his work are relatively eclipsed, such as the infinite qualitative distinction between God and humanity, the utterly unique nature of the revelation of God in Jesus Christ, the rejection of natural theology, and the dialectical character of Barth's theology. The result is an altogether more domesticated view of Barth's thought that fails to discern and inculcate some of the most radical, arresting

features of his work. For a number of reasons, this approach to Barth was the most easily digestible in the Anglo-American world during Barth's lifetime, and considerable cultural translation of the *Dogmatics* served to make Barth more acceptable in the English-speaking world. As one scholar puts it, a process of normalization occurred which adjusted and reformed certain aspects of Barth's thought to bring it into line with more acceptable conceptions of theology.[6] In short, the reading of Barth that was received into the English-speaking context, and the one that came to dominate the understanding of Barth's theology in that setting, was a reading and interpretation that was significantly shorn of its dialectical assumptions and character.

This neo-orthodox reading of Barth was also enabled by what became the most commonly accepted account of Barth's theological development, set forth and articulated in detail by the Catholic theologian Hans Urs von Balthasar in his important work on Barth's theology.[7] First published in German in 1951, von Balthasar's book suggests that there were two major shifts in Barth's thinking in the development of his theology. The first occurred in 1918 with his rejection of liberalism and move to a dialectical method of setting theological statements over against counterstatements without allowing a synthesis of the two to emerge. This approach led to Barth's highly influential commentary on Romans and is said to characterize his thinking until 1931. The publication of his work on Anselm in 1931 is then viewed as marking a second shift, this time from dialectic to analogy. The "turn to analogy" marks the point at which Barth abandons his dialectical method and adopts a more "objective" and "positivistic" approach to theology that comes to be known as neo-orthodoxy. Thus, we are presented with three phases in Barth's intellectual pilgrimage: the early, liberal Barth; the dialectical Barth; and the mature, neo-orthodox Barth of the *Church Dogmatics* who abandoned the dialectical method of his earlier thought. While this overall sequence has been nuanced in various ways, its basic form became established as the standard account of Barth's historical development and as the crucial background for interpreting the shape and content of his definitive theological statement in the *Church Dogmatics.*

A second, more recent interpretation of Barth moves in a direction that may be associated with certain aspects of postmodern thought and develops the theme of God as

"wholly other" that is accented in his early writings. The basic thrust of this approach suggests that finite human beings are simply incapable of describing the infinite God within the context of a single linguistic context, much less a particular theological system within a particular linguistic context. Proponents of this approach seek to bring Barth into conversation with postmodern philosophy. We will briefly mention two of these: the work of Walter Lowe[8] and that of Graham Ward[9] which bring Barth into conversation with the French postmodern linguistic and literary theorist Jacques Derrida and attempt to draw out affinities between the two.

Lowe focuses his attention on the second edition of Barth's Romans commentary, published in 1922, in which Barth calls into question all human theological complacency that assumes to have definitively settled the question of God and his relationship to the world. Lowe extends this early Barthian theme in tandem with the work of Derrida in order to develop an account of metaphysics that effectively renders the historical reality of the church's conception of God as fundamentally ambiguous. However, in developing his thesis, Lowe departs from interpretations of Derrida as a deconstructive nihilist with little interest in the question of truth. He demonstrates that Derrida is not a relativistic nihilist and that his thought cannot properly be employed in support of such purposes. Lowe suggests that the mistaken turn in much postmodern thought is that in its realization that truth could not be finally and completely grasped, it concluded that the very question of truth must be abandoned. He maintains that the question of truth is a reality that should not, and cannot, be disposed of, but rather needs to be recast in light of the contextual nature of the finite human condition. The purpose of Lowe's interpretation of Barth and Derrida is not simply to be deconstructive but also to open up new critical and constructive possibilities for theology on the basis of the radical otherness of God.

While Lowe looks to the early Barth of the second Romans commentary to develop his thesis, Graham Ward engages with the later Barth of the *Church Dogmatics* to discuss the challenges for theology created by an awareness of the inadequacy of human language to provide immediate access to reality. It is this "crisis of representation" that raises the question of God and the possibility of theology for Ward and provides the context from which he views the emergence of Barth's thought. He argues that the central challenge for Barth was to provide a theological account of the meaningfulness of language in general and to address specifically the question concerning the way in which the Word of God comes to expression in human words. However, according to Ward, Barth's attempt to resolve the problem of theological language, while suggestive of a way forward, finally ends in incoherence, leading him to appeal to Derrida as a thinker who supplies a "philosophical supplement" that may be added to Barth in order to give greater coherence to his conception of theological language. This linking of Derrida to Barth results in the construction of the conditions necessary for the development of a postmodern theology of the Word and human language. The result of this for Ward is a postmodern Barthianism in which the presence of God in human language is that of absence. In other words, what finite human beings are really able to "know" about God is his fundamental hiddenness and incomprehensibility. This emphasis on the radical otherness of God demands significant alterations to accounts of the theological task, whether liberal or conservative.

The Dialectical Barth

While each of these approaches to reading Barth can certainly point to passages in his writing that support the positions they seek to articulate, the question is whether or not they actually do justice to the contours of Barth's thought as a whole. Here the importance of Barth as a dialectical theologian comes into view. As we saw in the summary of the work of George Hunsinger in the previous chapter, Barth must be read as a dialectical theologian if we are to grasp the message that he attempted to convey concerning the direction and shape of theology that must always begin again at the beginning due to the nature of its unique subject. This dialectical approach to reading Barth implicitly raises questions concerning the legitimacy of the standard paradigm for interpreting his work. Hunsinger raises this issue, at least implicitly, in his suggestion that before responsible criticism of Barth can take place, "a more reliable depiction of the overall terrain, as well as of the proportional relationships among the various segments" must be secured.[10] While Hunsinger seeks to offer a fresh reading of Barth's theology, Bruce McCormack proposes a revised understanding of its historical beginnings and development that funds the interpretation offered by Hunsinger.[11]

In his work, McCormack provides detailed, meticulous, and erudite exposition of Barth's early works and the context in which they emerged that constitutes the most groundbreaking study of Barth in English-language interpretation. He maintains that after Barth's break with liberalism and the development of his dialectical conception of theology, there were no subsequent major shifts or turning points in his thinking. Dialectic was never simply left behind, as the formula suggesting a "turn from dialectic to analogy" implies. McCormack maintains that the great weakness of the construal of von Balthasar is that it conceals the extent to which Karl Barth remained a truly dialectical theologian, even in the *Church Dogmatics*. Thus, while Barth's theology certainly developed as he took on genuinely fresh insights, these were always maintained in the context of a fundamentally dialectical theology. Failure to recognize this has led to the domestication of Barth in the direction of overly positivistic neo-orthodox readings of his theology. Rather than neo-orthodox, Barth is a dialectical theologian whose thought is governed by the notion of indirect identity and the dialectic of veiling and unveiling discussed in the previous chapter. It is this dialectic of veiling and unveiling that drives Barth's entire approach to theology, to such an extent that failure to recognize it will inevitably lead to significant interpretive distortions.

Failure to grasp the ongoing dialectical character of Barth's theology is precisely the problem in both the neo-orthodox and postmodern readings of Barth that we have mentioned. The dialectic of veiling and unveiling is broken in each instance, albeit broken in different directions. In the case of neo-orthodoxy, the givenness of God in revelation is emphasized in such a way that Barth is potentially made into a revelational positivist who collapses the whole of revelation into the text of the biblical witness. In the case of the postmodern readings that stress the wholly otherness of God, the nongivenness and hiddenness of God in revelation is emphasized in such a way as to potentially turn Barth into a theological skeptic. The difficulty with both of these approaches is that they end up with an utterly and completely undialectical Barth. Hence, these interpreta-

tions are inadequate accounts of Barth's theology not because they have emphasized themes that are absent from Barth's writings, but rather because they have not taken adequate account of the whole, especially its dialectical character, in spite of the fact that they can indeed appeal to particular aspects of Barth's thought in support of the interpretations they offer.

What is the significance of this resurgence of interest in Barth for the practice of contemporary theology? As we noted earlier, the emerging postmodern context has triggered a quest for new theological paradigms that might more effectively address the contemporary situation in the aftermath of modernity. In this discussion, one of the central questions has to do with the compatibility of a biblical and confessional theology with some of the concerns of postmodernity. In short, is the idea of a robustly confessional theology that takes seriously the challenges of contemporary, postmodern culture simply oxymoronic or is it a genuine possibility? Barth's thought is highly suggestive of the potential contours of such a theology and may be taken to imply that it is not only possible but also desirable.

Barth did his work as a confessional theologian in the Reformed tradition who was chiefly concerned with exegetical and dogmatic questions. He thought and wrote as a biblical theologian who emphasized that God had spoken and could be known, while at the same time stressing the hiddenness of God and the ways in which revelation is never simply given over to human beings and never becomes subject to human control. He does raise questions concerning the nature of theological language that serve to unsettle both liberal and conservative approaches to theology. Further, the conclusions Barth draws in his explication of these topics do have some commonality with aspects of postmodern thought. What must be remembered is that Barth's

primary focus is theological rather than philosophical. This means that his development of these themes and his approach in addressing them is driven primarily by his concern to produce a biblical dogmatics that faithfully bears witness to the self-revelation of the living God.

The assertion that Barth's theology articulates some concerns held in common with postmodern theorists should not, however, lead to the conclusion that Barth was himself a postmodern thinker. While he certainly challenged aspects of modernity, it is also true that in many ways he remained a thoroughly modern theologian whose thought resonates with themes from the nineteenth century as well as with some of those of the late twentieth and early twenty-first. Barth is best viewed as a thinker who is able to speak to the postmodern situation not because he was a postmodern theologian but rather because he anticipated certain postmodern questions and concerns within the framework of a biblical dogmatics. Again, the problem with the neo-orthodox and postmodern readings of Barth is not that these themes and concerns have been found in Barth where they do not exist, but rather that they have not been articulated and developed within the method and framework of Barth's theology as a whole. Nevertheless, the presence of these themes suggests that their rearticulation within the context of Barth's dialectically conceived biblical dogmatics is a project brimming with fresh, constructive possibilities for a Christian theology that seeks to address the intellectual challenges raised by the emerging culture of the third millennium.

Conclusion: The Angels Laugh

Barth did not intend his theology to be an end in itself. Its aim was to bear witness to the God revealed in Jesus Christ and direct readers to consider the living subject of theology. Barth's work invites further investigation, with the hopeful expectation that there is always more to learn, rather like the vision of C. S. Lewis at the conclusion of his *Chronicles of Narnia*, where heaven, truth, and the knowledge of God are pictured metaphorically as involving an ongoing process of discovery that is facilitated through a journey that proceeds "further up and further in." The study of theology is an invitation to begin this never-ending pilgrimage into the grace, truth, and love of God. Hence, Barth was always somewhat amused by the amount of extended and detailed attention his theology received, as though its study and contemplation could be viewed as an end in itself.

"The angels laugh at old Karl. They laugh at him because he tries to grasp the truth about God in a book of Dogmatics. They laugh at the fact that volume follows volume and each is thicker than the previous one. As they laugh, they say to one another, 'Look! Here he comes now with his little pushcart full of volumes of the *Dogmatics*!'— and they laugh about the men who write so much about Karl Barth instead of writing about the things he is trying to write about. Truly, the angels laugh."[12]

Notes

2. Breaking with Liberalism

1. Eberhard Busch, *Karl Barth: His Life from Letters and Auto-biographical Texts* (Philadelphia: Fortress Press, 1976), 54.
2. Ibid.
3. Karl Barth, *The Humanity of God* (Atlanta: John Knox Press, 1960), 14.
4. Karl Barth, *The Theology of Schleiermacher* (Edinburgh: T. & T. Clark, 1982), 264.
5. Ibid.
6. Karl Barth, *The Word of God and the Word of Man* (London: Hodder & Stoughton, 1928), 37.
7. Busch, *Karl Barth*, 92, 97.

3. A New Theology

1. Karl Barth, *The Epistle to the Romans* (London: Oxford University Press, 1933), 2.
2. Ibid., 1.
3. Ibid., 10.
4. Barth, *Word of God*, 186.
5. Ibid., 272.
6. Ibid., 273.
7. Ibid., 277.
8. Ibid., 278.
9. Ibid., 281.
10. Ibid., 281–82.
11. Ibid., 282–83.
12. Ibid., 285.
13. Busch, *Karl Barth*, 111.

Notes

4. The Impossible Possibility

1. Eberhard Busch, *Karl Barth: His Life from Letters and Autobiographical Texts* (Philadelphia: Fortress Press, 1976), 126.
2. Ibid., 129.
3. Ibid., 127.
4. Ibid.
5. Ibid.
6. Ibid., 132.
7. Barth, *Word of God*, 186.
8. Ibid., 203.
9. Ibid., 204.
10. Ibid., 206.
11. Ibid., 207.
12. Ibid., 211.
13. Karl Barth, *Church Dogmatics* I/1:16 (Edinburgh: T. & T. Clark, 1975). (Hereafter cited as *CD*.)
14. Karl Barth, foreword to *Reformed Dogmatics,* by Heinrich Heppe (London: Allen & Unwin, 1950), v.
15. Ibid.
16. Ibid.
17. Karl Barth, *Göttingen Dogmatics: Instruction in the Christian Religion* (Grand Rapids: Wm. B. Eerdmans, 1991), 1:386.
18. Ibid., 1:294.
19. Ibid., 1:39.
20. Barth, *Word of God*, 169.
21. Barth, *Göttingen Dogmatics,* 1:270.
22. Ibid., 1:428.

5. Bearing Christian Witness

1. Karl Barth, *Theology and Church* (New York: Harper & Row, 1962), 282.
2. Ibid., 314.
3. Hans Urs von Balthasar, *The Theology of Karl Barth,* trans. Edward T. Oakes, SJ (San Francisco: Ignatius Press, 1992), 23.
4. Barth, *CD* I/1:xii–xiii.

5. Busch, *Karl Barth*, 217.

6. Timothy J. Gorringe, *Karl Barth: Against Hegemony* (Oxford: Oxford University Press, 1999), 119–20.

7. Busch, *Karl Barth*, 245.

8. John Leith, ed., *Creeds of the Churches*, 3rd ed. (Atlanta: John Knox Press, 1982), 520–22.

9. Busch, *Karl Barth*, 248.

10. Ibid., 255.

6. *Church Dogmatics*

1. Karl Barth, *Anselm: Fides Quaerens Intellectum* (London: SCM Press, 1960).

2. Karl Barth, *How I Changed My Mind* (Richmond: John Knox Press, 1966), 43–44.

3. Karl Barth, *Protestant Theology in the Nineteenth Century*, new ed. (Grand Rapids: Wm. B. Eerdmans, 2002), 3.

4. Karl Barth, *Dogmatics in Outline* (New York: Harper & Row, 1959), 9.

5. Barth, *CD* I/2:868.

6. John Webster, *Barth* (London: Continuum, 2000), 13–14.

7. George Hunsinger, *How to Read Karl Barth: The Shape of His Theology* (New York: Oxford University Press, 1991).

8. Ibid., vii.

9. Ibid., ix.

10. Ibid., viii.

11. Barth, *CD* I/1:3.

12. Ibid., 1:12.

13. Ibid., 1:23.

14. Webster, *Barth*, 57.

15. Barth, *CD* I/1:296.

16. Joseph L. Mangina, *Karl Barth: Theologian of Christian Witness* (Louisville, KY: Westminster John Knox Press, 2004), 37–38.

17. Barth, *CD* I/1:295.

18. Ibid., II/1:321.

19. Ibid., II/2:3.

20. Ibid., II/2:145.
21. Webster, *Barth,* 92.
22. Barth, *CD* II/2:509.
23. Ibid., III/1:3.
24. Ibid., 1:29.
25. Webster, *Barth,* 97–98.
26. Barth, *CD* III/1:43.
27. Webster, *Barth,* 98.
28. Barth, *CD* III/3:3.
29. Ibid., 3:12.
30. Mangina, *Karl Barth,* 99.
31. Barth, *CD* IV/1:ix.
32. Eberhard Busch, *The Great Passion* (Grand Rapids: Wm. B. Eerdmans, 2004), 52.
33. Barth, *CD* II/2:509.
34. Mangina, *Karl Barth,* 147.
35. Barth, *CD* II/2:568.
36. Webster, *Barth,* 155
37. Barth, *CD* II/2:576

7. Barth's Legacy

1. Busch, *Karl Barth,* 441.
2. Ibid., 487.
3. Ibid., 456.
4. Ibid., 489–90.
5. Hunsinger, *How to Read Karl Barth,* 27.
6. Richard Roberts, "The Reception of the Theology of Karl Barth in the Anglo-Saxon World: History, Typology and Prospect," in *Karl Barth: Centenary Essays,* ed. Stephen W. Sykes (Cambridge: Cambridge University Press, 1989), 125.
7. Balthasar, *Theology of Karl Barth.*
8. Walter Lowe, *Theology and Difference: The Wound of Reason* (Bloomington: Indiana University Press, 1993).
9. Graham Ward, *Barth, Derrida, and the Language of Theology* (Cambridge: Cambridge University Press, 1995).
10. Hunsinger, *How to Read Karl Barth,* x.

11. Bruce McCormack, *Karl Barth's Critically Realistic Dialectical Theology: Its Genesis and Development 1909–1936* (Oxford: Oxford University Press, 1995).
12. Karl Barth, quoted in Robert McAfee Brown, introduction to *Portrait of Karl Barth,* by George Casalis, (Garden City, NY: Doubleday, 1963), 3.

For Further Reading

The *Church Dogmatics*

Barth's unfinished magnum opus was originally published in German as *Die kirchliche Dogmatik* (1932–67). The authorized English translation is *Church Dogmatics,* 13 vols. (Edinburgh: T. & T. Clark, 1956–75). It should be noted that *CD* I/1 has appeared in two translations, one in 1936 and the other in 1975. Readers are advised to consult the 1975 translation of Geoffrey Bromiley. An important supplementary volume, *The Christian Life* (Edinburgh: T. & T. Clark, 1981), provides lecture fragments for the unfinished *CD* IV/4.

Other Selected Works by Barth

The Word of God and the Word of Man. Translated by Douglas Horton. London: Hodder & Stoughton, 1928.

The Epistle to the Romans. Translated by Edwyn C. Hoskyns. London: Oxford University Press, 1933.

The Resurrection of the Dead. Translated by H. J. Stenning. London: Hodder & Stoughton, 1933.

The Knowledge of God and the Service of God. Translated by J. L. M. Hare and Ian Henderson. London: Hodder & Stoughton, 1938.

Dogmatics in Outline. Translated by G. T. Thomson. London: SCM Press, 1960.

Anselm: Fides Quaerens Intellectum. Translated by Ian W. Robertson. London: SCM Press, 1960.

The Humanity of God. Translated by John Newton Thomas and Thomas Wieser. Atlanta: John Knox Press, 1960.

Theology and Church. Translated by Louise Pettibone Smith. New York: Harper & Row, 1962.

For Further Reading

Evangelical Theology: An Introduction. Translated by Grover Foley. New York: Holt, Rinehart & Winston, 1963.

Prayer and Preaching. Translated by Sara F. Terrien and B. E. Hooke. London: SCM Press, 1964.

Witness to the Word: A Commentary on John 1. Edited by Walther Furst. Translated by Geoffrey W. Bromiley. Grand Rapids: Wm. B. Eerdmans, 1986.

Prayer. Edited by Don E. Saliers. Translated by Sara F. Terrien. Louisville, KY: Westminster John Knox Press, 2002.

Epistle to the Philippians. Translated by James W. Leitch. Louisville, KY: Westminster John Knox Press, 2002.

Protestant Theology in the Nineteenth Century. New ed. Grand Rapids: Wm. B. Eerdmans, 2002.

Posthumously Published Academic Lecture Cycles

The Theology of John Calvin. Given in 1922. Translated by Geoffrey W. Bromiley. Grand Rapids: Wm. B. Eerdmans, 1995.

The Theology of the Reformed Confessions. 1923. Translated and annotated by Darrell L. and Judith J. Guder. Columbia Series in Reformed Theology. Louisville, KY: Westminster John Knox Press, 2002.

The Theology of Schleiermacher. 1923–24. Edited by Dietrich Ritschl. Translated by Geoffrey W. Bromiley. Edinburgh: T. & T. Clark, 1982.

The Göttingen Dogmatics: Instruction in the Christian Religion. 1924–25. Vol. 1. Edited by Hannelotte Reiffen. Translated by Geoffrey W. Bromiley. Grand Rapids: Wm. B. Eerdmans, 1991.

Ethics. 1928–29. Edited by Dietrich Braun. Translated by Geoffrey W. Bromiley. Edinburgh: T. & T. Clark, 1981.

Works concerning Barth

Balthasar, Hans Urs von. *The Theology of Karl Barth: Exposition and Interpretation.* Translated by Edward T. Oakes, SJ. San Francisco: Ignatius, 1992.

Busch, Eberhard. *Karl Barth: His Life from Letters and Autobiographical Texts.* Translated by John Bowden. Philadelphia: Fortress Press, 1976.

For Further Reading

———. *The Great Passion: An Introduction to Karl Barth's Theology*. Edited and annotated by Darrell L. and Judith J. Guder. Translated by Geoffrey W. Bromiley. Grand Rapids: Wm. B. Eerdmans, 2004.

Dorrien, Gary. *The Barthian Revolt in Modern Theology: Theology without Weapons*. Louisville, KY: Westminster John Knox Press, 2000.

Gorringe, Timothy J. *Karl Barth: Against Hegemony*. Oxford: Oxford University Press, 1999.

Hart, Trevor. *Regarding Karl Barth: Toward a Reading of His Theology*. Downers Grove, IL: InterVarsity Press, 1999.

Hunsinger, George. *How to Read Karl Barth: The Shape of His Theology*. New York: Oxford University Press, 1991.

———. *Disruptive Grace: Studies in the Theology of Karl Barth*. Grand Rapids: Wm. B. Eerdmans, 2000.

Johnson, William Stacy. *The Mystery of God: Karl Barth and the Postmodern Foundations of Theology*. Louisville, KY: Westminster John Knox Press, 1997.

Lowe, Walter. *Theology and Difference: The Wound of Reason*. Bloomington: Indiana University Press, 1993.

Mangina, Joseph L. *Karl Barth: Theologian of Christian Witness*. Louisville, KY: Westminster John Knox Press, 2004.

McCormack, Bruce L. *Karl Barth's Critically Realistic Dialectical Theology: Its Genesis and Development 1909–1936*. Oxford: Oxford University Press, 1995.

Richardson, Kurt Anders. *Reading Karl Barth: New Directions for North American Theology*. Grand Rapids: Baker Academic, 2004.

Ward, Graham. *Barth, Derrida, and the Language of Theology*. Cambridge: Cambridge University Press, 1995.

Webster, John. *Barth's Ethics of Reconciliation*. Cambridge: Cambridge University Press, 1995.

———. *Barth's Moral Theology: Human Action in Barth's Thought*. Grand Rapids: Wm. B. Eerdmans, 1998.

———, ed. *The Cambridge Companion to Karl Barth*. Cambridge: Cambridge University Press, 2000.

———. *Barth*. London: Continuum, 2000.

Index

actualism, 110–11
adoption by God, 48
age of reason, *See*
  Enlightenment
Althaus, Paul, 90
Altona declaration, 91
analogy, 112–13,
  156, 161
Anselm, 101–2, 156
anthropology, theo-
  logical, 130, 134
apostolic succession,
  81
Aryan paragraph, 91,
  92
atonement, *See* Jesus
  Christ: atonement

Balthasar, Hans Urs
  von, 83, 149,
  156, 161, 168
  n.3, 170 n.7
Barmen Declaration,
  93–97
Basel, 1, 26, 97, 99,
  151
being–in–act, 110,
  124, 140
Berlin, 2, 14, 92–93,
  97
Bern, 1, 2
Bethel Confession,
  92

Bible, 5, 19
  authority of, 7, 21
  God speaking
    through, 41
  inspiration of,
    41–42
  interpretation of,
    42, 103
  spirit of, 42
  "strange new
    world of," 36,
    39, 72
  study, 10, 33–38,
    41
  as symbolic docu-
    ments, 35
  understanding of,
    29
biblical exegesis,
  105–7, 113, 163
biblicism, 73, 106
Biefeld, Synod of,
  92
Bloody Sunday, 91
Blumhardt, Johann
  and Christoph,
  24, 25
Bonhoeffer, Dietrich,
  92
Bonn, 84, 86, 97,
  101, 106
Brown, R. M., 171,
  n.12

Busch, Eberhard,
  167 nn.1,7,13;
  168 nn.1–6; 169
  nn.5,7,9; 170 n.1

Calvin, John, 21–22,
  60, 63, 65,
  73–74, 149
Casalis, George, 171
  n.12
Catholic Church, 81,
  82, 90
Catholicism, 79, 82,
  90, 142
Center for Barth
  Studies, 152
Chalcedon, Council
  of, 22, 138
Christ, *See* Jesus
  Christ
Christian (term), 86
Christian Faith, The,
  14, 15
"Christian in society,
  The," 52–55
Christian socialism.
  See socialism:
  Christian/reli-
  gious
Christliche Welt, Die,
  4, 29
Christology. *See* Jesus
  Christ

Index

church, 80–81, 136
  authority of, 7
  delegitimization
    of, 46
  marks of, 82
  as primary audi-
    ence, x
  and state, 94–95
  tradition of, 7, 8,
    13, 17, 76,
    92, 101,
    102–3, 106–8,
    142–43, 149
  Church Dogmatics, x,
    85, 99–105,
    107–10, 115,
    117, 143, 149,
    151, 153, 157,
    159, 161, 168
    n.13
  shape of, 103–8
civilization, Christian,
  31
class conflict, 27
commandment. *See*
  God: command of
communion of saints,
  107
communism/-ists,
  24, 86–87, 90
community, 10, 118,
  142
  founded by
    Christ, 17
Confessing Church,
  93, 96
confession (s), 103,
  108, 120
covenant, 44, 47,
    117, 129–30,
    132–33, 135,
    142, 143
  fellowship, 145

of grace, 146–47
  See also grace
creation, 103
  consummation of,
    134
  doctrine of,
    130–36
  ethics of, 131
  God's new, 24,
    36
    See also God:
      kingdom of
  ongoing history
    of, 135
culture. *See* God: and
  culture

Derrida, Jacques,
  158–59
dialectic, 47–48, 50,
  108, 155–56
  theology. *See* the-
    ology: dialectic
dogma, 68
dogmatics, 28, 50,
    66–67
  biblical, 164–65
  criterion of, 105,
    118
  defined, 72, 117
  lectures on, 72,
    73, 77, 83,
    85, 150
  method, 101, 116
  serving the church,
    74, 100
  task of, 75, 86,
    108
Düsseldorf Theses,
  92

Eglersburg lectures,
  66, 72

election, 125,
  128–30, 135, 145
emotion, 15
Enlightenment, x,
  4–8, 115, 154
"eternal cornucopia,"
  150
ethics, 11, 17, 18,
    19, 21, 28,
    86, 129–30,
    136, 143–48
  See also creation:
    ethics of
Evangelical Reich
  Church, 90
experience, 6, 13
  Christian, 2, 19
  of salvation,
    10
  individual, 18, 19
  internal, 11
  religious, 15,
    35

faith, 7, 8, 19, 131–32
  eyes and ears of,
    123
  foundation of, 108
  and knowledge, 6,
    20, 113
  and modern
    world, xi
  questions of, 101
  rationality of, 100
  seeking under-
    standing, 101,
    103
feeling, 12
Francke, A. H., 10
Frankfurt, 93
freedom, 136
  loving in, 123–24,
    126–28, 143

Genesis, 130, 132
Geneva, 21–22
German
    Christians, 90–91
    Evangelical
        Church, 92, 94
God, 12, 103
    alone, 54, 78
    attributes of, 124
    of Bible, 7
    character of, 126
    command of,
        125, 130, 144,
        145, 147
    covenantal rela-
        tion. See
        covenant
    as creator, 44,
        131–32
    and culture,
        30–31, 52
    different from
        humanity, 31,
        40, 42–45,
        47–48, 77,
        126, 155, 158
    doctrine of,
        124–30
    domestication of,
        35
    election of. See
        election
    epistemic rela-
        tions, 123
    freedom of, 44–
        45, 63, 70, 77
    hiddenness of, 121,
        159, 163
    identity of, 112,
        126
    image of, 130,
        134
    as impotent, 26

incarnation, 118,
    136
is God, 77
judgment of, 46
kingdom of,
    24–26, 32–33,
    38, 46, 53, 55
    See also
    creation,
    God's new
knowledge of, 47,
    50, 75, 112,
    123, 125–26,
    130, 163, 165
movement of, 56
nature of, 107
objective reality
    of, 66
otherness of, 37,
    154–55, 159,
    162
promises of, 48
reality of, 125–26
relationship with,
    50, 111
rule of, 92
secularization of,
    52
self-revelation of,
    70, 101,
    112–13,
    118–20, 164,
    165
and society. See
    God: and cul-
    ture
Son of, 17,
    138–39
speak/talk about,
    44, 47–48,
    66–69, 120
    inability to,
    50, 66

understanding of,
    101
as "wholly other,"
    158
will of, 37, 47,
    70, 117, 129
witness to, 50,
    55, 107, 117,
    165
word of, 27, 34,
    63, 66, 70,
    76, 82, 94,
    103, 105,
    118–19,
    159
    doctrine of,
    115–23
    See also Bible:
    God speak-
    ing
    through
    works of, 126
gods in human
    image, 46
Gogarten, Friedrich,
    90
good, the, 143,
    145–46
Gorringe, T. J., 169
    n.6
Göttingen, 56,
    59–60, 65, 79,
    84
    dogmatics, 71–78
grace, 112–13,
    125–26, 129,
    140–42, 148,
    165
    electing, 145
    nature of, 81–82,
    140–42
Great War. See World
    War I

Index

Halle, University of, 11, 13
heaven, kingdom of. *See* God: kingdom of
Heidegger, Martin, 90
Heidelberg Catechism, 60, 62, 63
Heppe, Heinrich *Reformed Dogmatics*, 73, 168 n.14
Herrmann, Wilhelm, 3–4, 18–20, 21
Hirsch, Emanuel, 90
historical-critical method, 41–42
historical inquiry, 18, 19
history, 12, 19, 42, 95, 100
  Christian witness in, 30
  God and, 5, 55, 135
  study of, 80
  understanding of, 29
Hitler, Adolf, 57, 87, 88, 90–93, 96
Holy Spirit, 86, 117, 118, 136
  work of, 123, 125, 142
How to Read Karl Barth, 110
humanity, 134
  elevated status of, 5
  response to God, 44

See also anthropology, theological; God: different from humanity
Hunsinger, George, 109–10, 113–14, 160–61, 169 n.7, 170 nn.5, 10

ideologies, 78
idolatry, 45–46, 80
imago Dei, 134
incarnation. *See* God: incarnation
indirect identity, 121, 123
infinite qualitative distinction, 42

James, epistle of, 22
Jesus Christ
  atonement, 11
  centrality of, 19
  consciousness of God, 15
  cross of, 48, 136
  deity of, 6
  devotion to, 10
  experience of, 19
  faith in, 101, 132
  fellowship in, 135
  God revealed in, 48, 107
  humanity of, 17, 121–22, 134, 139
  lordship of, 24
  as mediator, 112
  message of, 27
  name of, 147
  obedience of, 138
  offices of, 138–40

orthodox understanding of, 22
  person, 15, 27
    and work, 136, 138–39
  proclamation of, 17
  resurrection of, 6, 54–55, 136
  revelation of God, 47, 122, 136
    in Scripture, 94, 106
  tradition of, 8
  two natures of, 129, 140, 142
Jews, 87–88, 90, 95–96
justification, 142

Kant, Immanuel, 8
Karl Barth Society, 152
Kierkegaard, Søren, 42
kingdom of God, 18
knowledge and faith. *See* faith: and knowledge
Kutter, Herrmann, 25–27, 32

language
  about God. *See* God: speech/talk about
  of apostles and prophets, 122
  of church, 117
  human, 48, 112–13, 117, 123, 159

inadequacy of, 50
theological, 113, 159, 163
law, 27
and gospel, 145, 147
moral, 6, 145
natural, 6, 145
See also God: command of
Leith, John, 169, n.8
Lewis, C. S., 165
Chronicles of Narnia, 165
liberalism. *See* theology: liberal
Lord's Prayer, 55
love, 124, 126–28, 165
See also freedom: loving in
Lowe, Walter, 158–59, 170 n.8
Lutheranism, 79, 89
Lutheran Church, 93–94
Luther, Martin, 74, 89, 149

Mangina, J. L., 169 n.16, 170 nn.30, 34
Marburg, 2, 3, 4, 20
Marxism, 26, 27
Marx, Karl, 25
McCormack, Bruce, 161, 171 n.11
metaphysics, 18, 158
miracles, 6
moral law, *See* law: moral

morality, 6, 11, 13, 18, 148
Moravians, 9, 10
Müller, Ludwig, 90
Münster, 79–80, 83–84
mysticism, 67
mythologies, 78

Napoleon, 13
nationalism, 24, 88, 89–90
National Socialism, 57, 58, 78, 86–87, 90–93, 96
Nazis, 88, 89–90, 92, 94–95
negation, 67–68
New Testament, lectures on, 61
Niemöller, Martin, 91
"No!," 75–76, 94
normalization, 156

objectivism, 112
On Religion, 11

"paragraphs," 104–5
particularism, 111–12
Pastor's Emergency league, 91
pattern recognition, 110, 115
Paul, Saint, 68
personalism, 112
philosophy, 100
Pietism, 10, 24
piety, 2, 11
poor, oppression of, 23

postmodern philosophy, 154, 158, 163, 165
theology. *See* theology: postmodern
practical ministry, 10
prayer, 10, 117
preaching, 10, 21, 31, 118–19
predestination, 129
Protestant(ism), x
cultural, 88
liberal, 79, 80, 82, 86
See also theology: liberal
modern, 115
neo-, 80
new, 83
orthodoxy, x, 155
progressive, 3
providence, 131, 135–36

Rade, Martin, 4, 29
Ragaz, Leonard, 25–27, 32, 51
rationalism, 13, 113
realism, 112–13
reason, 6, 7, 8, 19, 113
reconciliation, 103, 137, 142, 147
doctrine of, 136–43
redemption, 103
Reformation, 82–83
continual, 63
festival, 92
"Reformation as Decision, The," 92

Index

Reformed
  Church, 60, 63,
    93–94
  confessional tradi-
    tion, 65
  orthodoxy, 73, 75
  theologians, 92
  theology, 60–63,
    128, 143
  professor of,
    56, 60
  tradition, 73
Reformers, 68, 73
religion
  critique of, 46
  despisers of, 12
  essence of, 11
  a human phenom-
    enon, 55
  oppression by, 46
  philosophy of, 80
  self-legitimation
    of, 46
  universal impulse
    for, 13, 46
Renaissance, 5
retirement, 149
revelation
  actualistic charac-
    ter of, 123,
    162
  divine, 6–7, 103,
    116–17,
    118–22
  external, 6
  "givenness" of,
    154
  indirect, 123
  nature of, 155
  objective and sub-
    jective moment
    of, 123
  See also God: self-
    revelation of

Ritschl, Albrecht,
    16–19, 73
Ritschlianism, 17, 19
Roberts, Richard,
    170 n.6
Romans, Epistle of,
    38, 44
  Commentary on,
    39–48, 51, 56,
    72, 149, 156,
    158
Romanticism, 13

Safenwil, 22, 39, 59,
    65
  "Red" pastor of,
    22–23, 28
salvation, 24, 133,
    136, 142
sanctification, 142,
    145
Schleiermacher,
    Friedrich,
    8–15, 18, 61,
    73, 75, 149
  Christian Faith,
    The, 14, 15
  On Religion, 11
  Speeches on Reli-
    gion, 13, 14,
    15, 19
science, 12–13, 19,
    62, 108
Scripture, 121
  authority of, 6
  basic to dogmat-
    ics, 72
  Catholic under-
    standing of, 81
  human authorship
    of, 34
  inspiration of, 6
  listening to, 101
  nature of, 34–35

quotations, 94
unity of, 113
witness of, 108,
    136
  See also Bible
Seeberg, Reinhold, 90
self-criticism, 67–68
sermons. See preach-
    ing
sin, 136, 140–41
social
  democrats, 23,
    24, 88
  gospel, 24
  responsibility, 24
socialism, 24
  Christian/reli-
    gious, 24–27,
    32, 38, 50–51
society, 53, 86
  See also God: and
    culture
speech. See language
speech-act, 119
Speeches on Religion,
    13, 15, 19
Spener, P. J., 10
spirit, human, 86
state, the, 94–95
superstition, 6
Sykes, S. W., 170 n.6

Tambach lecture,
    50–56, 72
teleology, 132
Ten Commandments,
    21, 45
theology, 151, 163
  biblical, x, 102,
    163
  Catholic, 80
  compendiums of,
    75
  confessional, 163

Index

conservative, ix, 2, 3, 10
counter-intuitive, 100
dialectic, 66, 68–70, 102, 108, 113–15, 155, 160–61
    See also dialectic
freestyle, 42
goal of, 70
impossible possibility of, 66–70, 72
liberal, ix, x, 2, 4, 11, 15, 34, 38
    break with, 23, 31, 38, 39, 156, 161
    development of, 16–20
    end of, 28–33
    modern Protestant, 112
    nineteenth century, 29
    in sermons, 22
natural, 125–26, 155
neo-orthodox, 154–57, 161–62, 165
new form of, x, 49, 154
positive, 2, 156
postmodern, 157–59, 162, 164–65
reconstruction of, 39
scholastic, 75

task of, 63
Trinitarian, 118
twentieth century, ix–x
as witness, 165
Thomas Aquinas, 150
Thurneysen, Eduard, 33
tradition
    Catholic, 79, 81, 83
    Christian, 102–3, 106
    Reformed, 60–61, 62–63, 65, 73, 149, 163
    witness of, 108
    See also church: tradition of
Trinity, 118, 121, 124, 133, 134, 144
truth, 6, 34, 140, 158, 165–66
    of Christianity, 19
    fragmentary, 68–69
    about God, 101, 118
    living, 68
    moral, 147
    of religious faith, 19
    ultimate, 46
Tübingen, 2, 3
tutelage, 8

ultimate reality, 15, 70
unions, trade, 27

veiling and unveiling, 121, 123, 161–62

Versailles Treaty, 57, 89
vocation, 142

war
    guilt clause, 57–58
    ideology of, 32, 44
    legitimacy of, 29, 31
Ward, Graham, 158–59, 170 n.9
Webster, John, 169 nn.6, 14; 170 nn.21, 25, 27, 36
Weimar
    constitution, 86
    Republic, 58, 87
witness
    to God. See God: witness to
    to gospel, 63
    to humanity, 77
Word. See God: word of
Word of God and the Word of Man, The, 66
"Word of God as the Task of Theology, The," 66
words, human. See language: human
working class, 27
world-principle, 128
World War I, 23, 28–29, 50, 89

Zinzendorf, Nikolaus von, 9–10
Zwingli, Huldrych, 61, 73